LEADING WOMEN

Queen Noor

PAMELA DELL

Cavendish Square

New York

S

Published in 2014 by Cavendish Square Publishing, LLC
303 Park Avenue South, Suite 1247, New York, NY 10010

First Edition

Website: cavendishsq.com

This publication represents the opinions and views of the author based on his or her personal experience, knowledge, and research. The information in this book serves as a general guide only. The author and publisher have used their best efforts in preparing this book and disclaim liability rising directly or indirectly from the use and application of this book.

CPSIA Compliance Information: Batch #WS13CSQ

All websites were available and accurate when this book was sent to press.

Library of Congress Cataloging-in-Publication Data
Dell, Pamela.
Queen Noor / Pamela Dell.
p. cm. (Leading women)
Includes bibliographical references and index.
ISBN 978-0-7614-4958-4 (hardcover)—ISBN 978-1-62712-116-3 (paperback)
—ISBN 978-1-60870-715-5 (ebook)
1. Noor, Queen, consort of Hussein, King of Jordan, 1951—Juvenile literature. 2. Queens—Jordan
Biography—Juvenile literature. 3. Middle East—History—20th century—Juvenile literature. 4. Arab-Israeli
conflict—Juvenile literature. I. Title.
DS154.52.N87D45 2012
956.9504'4092—dc22 [B]
2010042006

Editor: Deborah Grahame-Smith   Art Director: Anahid Hamparian   Series Designer: Nancy Sabato
Photo research by Connie Gardner

Cover art by Katie Travelstead

All other photographs in this book are used by permission and through the courtesy of: *Getty Images*:
Sean Gallup, 1; Khalil Mazraw, 4; Larry Dalton, 27; Travel Ink, 34; David Hume Kennerly, 42, 58;
Sahm Doherty, 53; Tom Stoddard, 71; Roger Violett, 82; David Montgomery, 86; Terry O'Neil, 89;
Ralph Alswang, 95; Paul Richards, 101; *Corbis*: Corbis Edge, 10; Nathan Benn, 65; *AP Photo*: 4, 24, 46,
Sipa 43, Jim Rogash, 104; *The Image Works*: Silvio Fiore 38; Topham, 74; *Mudd Manuscript Library*, 32.

Printed in the United States of America

CONTENTS

CHAPTER 1

A Woman Who Would Be Queen 4

CHAPTER 2

Youthful Awakening 10

CHAPTER 3

Path to the Middle East 24

CHAPTER 4

Connecting with a King 38

CHAPTER 5

Jordan's New Queen 46

CHAPTER 6

Making a Difference 58

CHAPTER 7

Conflict in the Middle East 74

CHAPTER 8

Balancing Public and Private Life 86

CHAPTER 9

Continuing Contributions 104

TIMELINE 114

SOURCE NOTES 116

FURTHER INFORMATION 122

BIBLIOGRAPHY 123

INDEX 126

CHAPTER ONE

A Woman Who Would Be Queen

I N JULY 2009, NEARLY 140 TEENS FROM seventeen countries gathered in the Middle East to attend an eye-opening event. Their destination was Amman, the capital of Jordan. They traveled not only from surrounding Arab nations and territories, but also from places as far-flung as Italy, Indonesia, France, Pakistan, Russia, and the United States.

These dedicated young people, ranging in age from fourteen to sixteen, were in Amman to attend the twenty-ninth annual International Arab Children's Congress (IACC). The purposes of this yearly event are numerous. First, it provides a powerful opportunity for youth to express their concerns and aspirations to the leaders of the Arab world. The teens also have a chance to share their ideas about important issues like women's rights, the environment, and climate change.

Another vital aim of this conference is to further cross-cultural understanding among youth. Every year, teens from very different cultures and lifestyles have an opportunity to make friends and to break down stereotypes. The conference also offers young people a chance to expand their understanding of the principles of democracy and human rights. The result is a life-changing experience—one that suggests a glimmer of hope for the possibility of true world peace.

A GUIDING LIGHT

The goals of the IACC are backed by an inspiring vision. Its founder is someone whose lifework has focused on bringing aid

The annual International Arab Children's Conference, established by Queen Noor, draws young people to Amman, Jordan, from countries throughout the world.

to people in need and promoting peace. That person is Queen Noor Al Hussein, widow of the late King Hussein of Jordan. An American-born woman who was christened Lisa Najeeb Halaby, Queen Noor has lived in two extremely different worlds. She grew up and came of age in the United States. Today she again spends much time in her country of birth, but for most of her adult life she has lived in Jordan, a small nation bordered by Syria, Iraq, Saudi Arabia, and Israel.

Jordan has often been like the eye of the storm of conflict that characterizes the Middle East. As a result, Queen Noor understands firsthand the critical need to bridge the gap among different cultures. And she has been working tirelessly throughout her life to do something about that need.

A PATH OF DESTINY

As a girl, Lisa Halaby probably didn't expect to marry a king when she grew up. But when that unusual event occurred, on June 15, 1978, the press had a field day. They could not get enough of this rare and glamorous storybook romance.

All the parts were in place to make a perfect fairy tale: A tall, beautiful, blonde American, only twenty-six years old, is invited to lunch at the palace of the widowed forty-two-year-old Jordanian king. He is soon smitten. Within only a few weeks he asks her to be his wife. She says yes.

This is the ultrashort story. But like any intriguing tale, the deeper, fuller version shows how chance and fortunate circumstances sometimes lead to an unexpected destiny. It also reveals the fact that life for the king and queen of Jordan wasn't all a blissful fairy tale. As well as romance, there was a great deal of struggle on many levels for the king and his American queen.

THE INTERNATIONAL ARAB CHILDREN'S CONGRESS

"By bringing together young people from all over the world at a stage in their lives when they can begin to appreciate common values within their diverse perspectives," Queen Noor has said about the annual IACC, "we hope to lay the groundwork for a more respectful and cooperative world."

Queen Noor was inspired to organize the annual congress after the Arab Summit Conference of 1980, which brought together Arab leaders in Amman, Jordan. Her vision was to give young people the chance to express their ideas, grievances, hopes, and fears in a way similar to what occurred at the Arab Summit. By speaking out, Noor believes, young people may get their nations' leaders to notice—and to listen. The IACC became an international event in 2004, when the conference was opened to students from Europe and Asia as well as Arab countries.

PROGRESSIVE JORDAN

The country of Jordan has a distinct air of modernity. While much of its population lives in poverty, its citizenry also includes many well-educated, sophisticated, middle-class inhabitants. It's a city with lots of trees, flower gardens, and parks. Street cleaning and garbage collection occur on a regular basis. There are streetlights throughout town, as well as good water and sewage systems.

A constitutional monarchy, Jordan is also a more open society than many Middle Eastern nations. The king is the most powerful member of the government, but the country operates under a constitution established in 1952, a few months after the death of King Hussein's grandfather, King Abdullah I. Abdullah was exceptionally progressive compared to other Middle Eastern leaders of his time, and his ideas deeply influenced his grandson.

Although the king remains the ultimate power, Jordanian citizens elect their members of parliament. Both men and women have voting rights, and the first nationwide elections were held in 1967. Because of political and constitutional difficulties, elections did not resume until 1989, but both elections were considered unusually free and fair. "It's not a democracy," Queen Noor told a reporter shortly after her marriage, "but at the same time it's a monarchy based on a parliament that is elected. . . . So its legal definition is one that is not so far removed from a democracy."

By the time Lisa Halaby met King Hussein, cultural forces and life experiences had already shaped her in significant ways. She rose to the continual challenges with courage and grace. At the time of her marriage, some might have doubted that Jordan's new queen would make a name for herself. But now, a few decades later, Queen Noor is universally recognized. People admire and respect her for her countless humanitarian accomplishments and contributions to the world. Many consider her a true trailblazer in her wide-ranging work in service to humanity.

This is her remarkable story.

CHAPTER TWO

Youthful Awakening

I T WAS A MOMENT OF FEAR AND THEN helpless guilt for the ten-year-old girl on her pony. Roaming the countryside on horseback near her grandmother's Virginia farm with a friendly German shepherd tagging along, she had few worries. She came from a well-to-do family. She attended the best schools, and all her material needs were easily met. But she was hardly expecting to come across a row of badly run-down shacks just beyond her grandmother's property.

Gathered there was a group of migrant farmworkers and their children. To young Lisa they presented a picture of utter poverty and hopelessness. As she passed by, the workers regarded her with what she later recalled as "blank, hopeless stares." Lisa's shock and guilt struck deep. It was, perhaps, the first awakening of her social conscience. Never in her ten privileged years had she come across such obvious misery so up close or personally. It made a deep impression that ultimately developed into a strong desire to help people.

TRADITIONAL PARENTS

Lisa Najeeb Halaby was born August 23, 1951, in Washington, D.C., far removed in space and time from her future as a queen. Her parents, Najeeb Halaby and Doris Carlquist, were idealistic young people who met in D.C. in fall 1945. World War II had ended recently, and both parents held good jobs. So the Halabys' life

Young Lisa Halaby's first humanitarian impulses sprung from an encounter with migrant workers while she was horseback riding.

was already very comfortably middle class at the time of Lisa's birth.

Both of her parents had traditional upbringings, although different. The American-born only child of an American mother and a father of Syrian descent, Najeeb Halaby grew up in Texas. His parents were wealthy and successful, so Najeeb was well educated and got the best of everything.

Doris, whose heritage was Swedish, was from Spokane, Washington. Her father lost his business in the stock market crash of 1929, and Doris was unable to finish college for financial reasons.

Unlike most people raised in Syria, who are Muslims, Najeeb's ancestors belonged to the country's small minority of Christians. Doris was also a Christian. Not long after meeting and falling in love, the couple married on the Christmas Eve of 1945.

After Lisa's birth, the Halabys followed the accepted and traditional path of married couples in the 1950s. Doris left her job as an administrative assistant in the U.S. State Department. She took on the conventional stay-at-home role that was common among women of her time. Her primary goals were to raise her newborn daughter and to run a household.

The Halaby family soon grew. In 1953, Lisa's brother, Christian, was born, followed by her sister, Alexa, in 1955. They were the children of typical upper-middle-class parents, who aspired to do well economically, to provide for their children, and to maintain a level of high social status. They were also the children of a father who expected perfection.

FAMILY ON THE MOVE

Even as a newlywed, Najeeb Halaby had burning career goals. These goals were fueled by his lifelong passion for and experience in the field of aviation. A self-proclaimed workaholic, Najeeb, nicknamed Jeeb, spent little time involved in family life. Before Lisa was even born, he had joined a new branch of the U.S. State Department and had served as a civil aviation adviser to the king of Saudi Arabia. This not only increased Jeeb's passion for his chosen field. It also furthered his deep interest in the Middle East, where his father's roots lay.

After working his way through a series of important posts in the federal government, Najeeb set his sights on finding a corporate position. Ambitious and driven, he knew he could make a better salary in the business world. Jeeb's opportunity came shortly after Lisa's birth, when Eastern Airlines in New York offered him a job. It was just the type of nongovernmental opportunity the young father was looking for.

In 1953, when Lisa was two, the Halaby family relocated from D.C. to Manhattan's affluent Upper East Side. But just three years later, Jeeb quit the airline and took a new job in Los Angeles, California. At only five, Lisa, along with her siblings, was bound for another major relocation. Many more moves followed as their father's career took him from one position to the next, from one city to another.

Every time Najeeb uprooted the family, young Lisa had to adjust once again. These constant changes were difficult. Before long, she had developed a case of extreme shyness. In her young girl's mind, she was a permanent outsider plopped down time and again on unfamiliar turf.

It didn't help that Lisa's parents did not seem to understand her social awkwardness or where it came from. Her mother worried that her first daughter was too much of a loner. Her perfection-seeking father expected as much from his daughter as he did of himself. And to him, Lisa's inability to adapt quickly to ever-changing circumstances was far from a perfect trait. In Jeeb's opinion, his daughter was cold and unapproachable. He didn't understand that she was simply shy in new circumstances.

SWEET HOME CALIFORNIA

In California, however, Lisa began to feel happier. Although the family lived in a series of different houses and different neighborhoods, the Pacific Ocean was never far away. Lisa liked being outside in the year-round balmy weather. A strong swimmer, she loved going to the beach and playing in the salty surf. The ocean provided two things she really desired—a challenge and a sense of freedom.

Lisa had other favorite pastimes as well. She loved horseback riding and was an avid reader. She got a quiet enjoyment out of exploring the natural world around the Halaby house. She also loved spending time with her artistic paternal grandmother, Laura Halaby, who accompanied the family every time they moved to a new city.

For five mostly blissful years, Lisa enjoyed an affluent life in Southern California. But in 1961, things changed again. In January of that year, she and her siblings watched the inauguration of the new president, John F. Kennedy, on TV in their Los Angeles home. But their parents were not there with them. Instead, Najeeb and Doris Halaby were clearly visible on the television screen as part of the group seated behind President Kennedy. They had been invited to the inauguration ceremony because Kennedy had appointed Najeeb head of an important new department of the government, the Federal Aviation Agency.

Today known as the Federal Aviation Administration (FAA), this governmental agency oversees all aspects of U.S. civil aviation. Formed in 1958, the FAA was still so new when Jeeb took over that

President Kennedy watches as Najeeb Halaby is sworn in as administrator of the Federal Aviation Agency on March 3, 1961.

he was only its second director. It was a high-prestige position but a low-paying one. By agreeing to take the job, Jeeb was agreeing to a salary only about one-third what he had made in the private sector. Also, the new job required him to be back in Washington, D.C. Another move for the Halabys was on the horizon.

AWAKENING SOCIAL CONSCIENCE

Leaving the ever-present ocean and Southern California sunshine for the chilly weather and more formal lifestyle on the East Coast was not easy for Lisa. Her shyness was still a hurdle to be overcome.

GLIMPSES OF THINGS TO COME

On a single day in California, before her family moved back to Washington, D.C., Lisa Halaby learned a number of new things. She discovered the thrill of flying in helicopters. She realized her father was an important man in the U.S. government. And she found out she had a fear of appearing in public.

All of these things were revealed to her in the day's events. The first was a going-away party held in honor of her father at the classy Ambassador Hotel in Los Angeles. Instead of driving to the party, the Halabys were flown there in a government helicopter. After the party, they took another helicopter ride to the brand-new Los Angeles International Airport. There, Jeeb was in charge of a special ceremony, officially opening the airport for business.

A special guest was in attendance at this ceremony, too. This was Vice President Lyndon B. Johnson. His role was to unveil a plaque to commemorate the airport's opening. But he wasn't alone onstage for this historic moment. Unbeknownst to Lisa, someone had arranged for her to stand up there with Johnson. She was horrified to discover this, but she pulled off her first public appearance with grace and poise. She even received compliments later from the vice president's wife, Lady Bird Johnson. Little did Lisa know then that within less than two decades, she would be on the world stage—and traveling a great deal by helicopter. At not even ten years old, she was already getting a taste of what her life would be like as an adult.

And she was, she has said,

Tall for my age, scrawny and awkward, and dependent on Coke-bottle-thick glasses.

Once again, Lisa had to confront the reality of being a stranger in a strange land. But as always, her grandmother Laura had moved along with her son's family. Now Laura Halaby lived in a place that was Lisa's great escape. That place was a farm in the nearby Virginia countryside, where Lisa could indulge her love of horseback riding. It was also the place where she had that first glimpse of true poverty, when she encountered the local farmworkers.

That shocking sight undoubtedly drove Lisa's earliest ideas about how to help people. She has noted that her number one career goal during the time she lived in D.C. was to join the Peace Corps.

Even at her young age, Lisa was taking to heart the famous line from President Kennedy's inaugural speech: "Ask not what your country can do for you. Ask what you can do for your country." One thing was holding her back from joining the Peace Corps, however. Volunteers had to be at least eighteen years old to sign up. She still had a few years before she could seriously consider it.

Lisa would have preferred to spend those years in public school, but her parents weren't willing to consider that option. For the Halaby children, getting educated in Washington, D.C., meant attending upscale private schools. With Jeeb's greatly reduced income and Doris's unemployment, this was hardly easy to afford. But it was nevertheless a priority for Lisa's parents. Lisa was enrolled at the National Cathedral School, which she attended through eighth grade.

PRESIDENT KENNEDY'S PEACE CORPS

For Lisa, joining the Peace Corps was a natural and timely goal. President Kennedy had established the organization in March 1961. The aim of the Peace Corps is "to promote world peace and friendship" by sending thousands of U.S. citizen volunteers all over the world. Since the organization's founding, Peace Corps workers have volunteered in almost 150 countries. One important mission is to bridge the culture gap. Another is to help developing nations improve their agricultural, educational, and technological systems.

CIVIL RIGHTS AWAKENING

The pressure to live up to their father's expectations was a powerful force in the lives of the Halaby children. Jeeb had high standards, and he wasn't one to ease up. He prided himself on raising independent, individualistic children. But he also expected them to excel as he saw fit. More and more, Lisa wanted to be accepted for who she was, not who she was expected to be.

Lisa was becoming an aware young girl with a greater and greater social conscience. In 1961, at only ten, she joined the Student Nonviolent Coordinating Committee (SNCC). SNCC was an organization whose young members worked tirelessly to end social injustice and to promote civil rights. Lisa attended SNCC events and participated in protest marches. She was proud of her involvement.

In the fall of 1962, Lisa watched as TV broadcasts showed a young African-American man named James Meredith attempting to enroll at the University of Mississippi. A violent backlash broke out among racist whites, who did everything they could to keep Meredith out. Mississippi governor George Wallace even defied federal law in his attempts to prevent Meredith from enrolling.

On TV, Lisa saw Meredith being escorted across campus by federal agents who were there to ensure his safety. She was shocked and upset to discover that her grandmother, who was watching with her, supported Mississippi's racist governor, not Meredith.

After this dramatic scene, a new face filled the television screen. For the first time, Lisa saw the celebrated religious and civil rights leader Dr. Martin Luther King speak. The minister's profound words about the hatred directed toward Meredith made a lasting impression on her. It awakened her interest in civil rights and further strengthened her humanitarian ideals.

On August 28, 1963, only five days after she turned twelve, Lisa had another opportunity to feel Dr. King's powerful impact. A crowd of more than 200,000 gathered at Washington's Lincoln Memorial. Known as the March on Washington, this massive civil rights demonstration was organized to highlight issues of "jobs and freedom." It was here that Dr. King gave his world-famous "I have a dream" speech. The civil rights leader's message fired the political spirit of thousands of young Americans, including Lisa. As the acclaimed singer and songwriter Bob Dylan put it, "The times they [were] a-changing."

TRAGEDY STRIKES

It was a time of turmoil and growing unrest. And on November 22, 1963, another dramatic event rocked the nation. That afternoon, tragic news spread through National Cathedral School and across the country. America's dynamic young president had been assassinated in Dallas, Texas. Kennedy had been shot in the head while his motorcade was traveling a parade route through the Dallas streets. A man who had inspired millions of people, including Lisa and her parents . . . was gone. Lisa remembers:

" President Kennedy's death shattered my world. His assassination was a crushing blow, especially after such a heady period of optimism and hope. "

After Kennedy's death, Vice President Lyndon Johnson was sworn in as the new president. Though much had suddenly changed at the top levels of the government, Najeeb Halaby was still in charge of the FAA. But now he wanted to leave government work and return to the corporate world. He tried to resign many times. Each time, President Johnson refused his resignation. At last, in 1965, Johnson finally agreed to let Jeeb go. It was time for yet another move.

BACK TO MANHATTAN

At fourteen, Lisa had to try to fit in once again in a new place. She had spent her earliest years in New York City, but she had no memories

HEART TO HEART

In her memoir, *Leap of Faith: Memoirs of an Unexpected Life*, Queen Noor recounts an incident from her childhood in Washington, D.C. She remembers a time when her father un-expectedly confided in her. He confessed that, even though his limited governmental salary had put him deeply in debt, he felt happier in public service than anywhere else. Queen Noor wrote, "The conversation . . . had a profound impact on my thinking, my dreams for the future, and my appreciation for sacrifices made for a larger purpose." The dedication of both her parents to serving the public good has guided Queen Noor's choices throughout her life since then.

of that Manhattan. Now about to enter high school, she visited a num-ber of schools with her parents. She had strong ideas about the kind of school she wanted to attend. The school her parents chose, however, was her very last choice. That school was the super-exclusive Chapin School of New York City.

The Halabys had returned to Manhattan because Jeeb had taken a new job as head of Pan-American Airlines. Now, although he was in debt from his years of government service, he could afford the high tuition for private school. Chapin, an all-girls school, had a presti-gious reputation and a long history of providing quality education. It would also, Lisa's parents believed, keep her away from the worst effects of peer pressure.

Lisa resisted her parents' decision. Few high schools could have suited her—a girl who valued her own individuality—less. Chapin was steeped in old-time tradition. Girls were required to dress like "proper ladies." In earlier years, this had included wearing white gloves and hats. By the time Lisa started her freshman year, gloves were no longer part of the dress code—but hats remained. Girls also had to endure checks on the length of their skirts. If the skirt didn't skim the floor when a girl knelt down, it was too short. The incoming fashion craze—miniskirts—was absolutely not an option. And no one would have even considered pants!

Worse than the rigid and old-fashioned dress code was the insulation from the "real world." Girls at Chapin generally came from wealthy and important families. They did not represent a range of ethnic backgrounds. Tuition was so costly that only the richest families could afford to send their daughters there.

In the mid-1960s, Chapin students were kept in a virtual bubble. Civil rights issues brewed across America. The United States had entered the Vietnam War, a brutal conflict between communist North Vietnam and non-communist South Vietnam. Opposing opinions about the war were dividing American citizens. But inside Chapin School, it was as if none of these events were even taking place.

A WELCOME CHANGE OF SCENE

For once, making a move was not something to dread. After two years at Chapin School, Lisa had had enough. Like a flower planted in the wrong type of soil, she wasn't growing properly. She was determined to finish high school somewhere better suited to her.

That better place, Lisa decided, was Concord Academy. Concord was a private boarding school in Concord, Massachusetts. At first her parents refused to consider letting her transfer out of Chapin. But Concord, at the time an all-girls school, was considered one of the

CHAPIN SCHOOL

Maria Bowen Chapin founded Chapin School in 1901. At that time, women still did not have the right to vote. Chapin, however, had been an active suffragette—an outspoken champion of legalizing voting for women. Ironically, at the time Lisa attended, the student body at Chapin moved within a web of rules and restrictions. Speaking out on controversial issues of the day, as Chapin had, was strictly forbidden. This was especially true if a student's beliefs or opinions happened to challenge the establishment—the traditional order of things.

This certainly described Lisa. She supported equal rights for all people, no matter their skin color. She was outspoken about her belief that the Vietnam War was wrong and should be ended. Living in Washington, she had been at the heart of the action. Now, at Chapin, it was more like being on a remote island, far removed from the upheaval of the world. For a young activist like Lisa, this lack of political dialogue was completely stifling.

top high schools in the nation. Its excellent academic record attracted stellar students from all over. Given these facts, Lisa finally got her wish. Before her junior year, her parents agreed to let her finish school there.

In an atmosphere that emphasized intellectual challenge and the importance of being an individual, the future queen had finally found her place. Now she would begin determining how she could best serve the world.

CHAPTER THREE

Path to the Middle East

CALIFORNIA WAS CALLING. IT WAS 1969, and Lisa was a few months from graduating high school. She had long since mapped out her college plans. Now she was eagerly looking forward to fulfilling them.

If all went the way she expected it to, she would go to yet another liberal and prestigious school. That school was Stanford University in Palo Alto, where her father had gone. Palo Alto was a sun-soaked town on the California coast south of San Francisco. She would be back in the state where she had been happy as a girl. As well as her studies, Lisa would have the beach, horseback riding, and plenty of political action.

In fall 1969, however, a big change was happening at a school much closer to home. Princeton University, a top Ivy League school in New Jersey, was doing something it hadn't done in its previous 222 years of existence. It was planning to admit women.

Encouraged by her high school counselor, Lisa had applied to Princeton as well as Stanford. She had barely even taken it seriously, however. It was Stanford she had her heart set on. She had had enough of the straight-laced, much-less-sunny East Coast. But she was stopped in her tracks when Princeton—as well as Stanford—accepted her. Which school would she choose?

PRINCETON YEARS

Choosing a university was a big dilemma. In the end, though, Lisa let go of her California dream. Instead, she chose Princeton

Students at Princeton University relaxing on the grass in 1970—
a turbulent year at American universities

over Stanford. Being part of Princeton's first coeducational class was clearly a historic opportunity—one she did not want to let slip away.

On September 6, 1969, Lisa was one of just 171 young women to break Princeton's long-established all-male boundary. One hundred of these women were new freshmen. The rest were transfer students from other colleges. In a freshman class of 921, the female minority was hard to miss. The young women's unique presence at Princeton caused a media frenzy. Journalists from every type of outlet swarmed the school to get photos and interviews.

It was a good story. The women's movement was just getting under way. When people thought of doctors, lawyers, or bankers, they thought of them as men. But the new women students at Princeton were not there to learn how to be good housewives. They had ambitions as strong as those of their male counterparts. And they were equally concerned with the issues of the day.

Princeton's activist-oriented environment suited Lisa. And she felt right at home—as an equal—with the male portion of the student body. "I was totally and utterly spoiled by growing up in a family and in schools and among friends . . . who didn't treat women any differently than men," she told a reporter long after becoming queen of Jordan. "In my own mind it never occurred to me that my gender would be a barrier to me."

WIDESPREAD PROTEST

By 1969, the counterculture—members of society who want to see big social and political changes—was alive and well. This was especially true on college campuses throughout the country. At Princeton, the outcry against the Vietnam War was loud, and for Lisa the war was the issue that took center stage. It wasn't exactly the path

Students protest the Vietnam War at the University of California,
Los Angeles, in April 1972.

her mother had anticipated. Doris Halaby tried unsuccessfully to per-
suade Lisa to follow the upper-class tradition of coming out, or being
formally introduced into society. Part of this ritual included attending
a series of ritzy New York City debutante balls—hardly Lisa's style.
While her mother was trying to coax her daughter into buying a ball
gown and long white gloves, Lisa was wearing a black armband and
joining passionate antiwar protests on campus.

In October 1969, a massive crowd of more than 250,000 people staged a demonstration against the war in Washington, D.C. At
Princeton, Lisa and other students fasted as part of their own Vietnam Moratorium Day. She joined in other protests as well.

THE VIETNAM WAR: 1961 TO 1975

The United States got involved in the Vietnam conflict because communism appeared to be on the move. The U.S. objective was to keep communism from spreading further by preventing communist North Vietnam from taking over the non-communist state of South Vietnam, which was centered in Saigon. Author Philip Caputo wrote in his 1977 book *A Rumor of War: Marine Officer in Vietnam*:

"War is always attractive to young men who know nothing about it. We were persuaded to go into uniform by Kennedy's challenge to 'Ask what you can do for your country.' The USA had never lost a war and it seemed we were [destined] to play cop to the communist robber and spread our political ideas around the world. . . . Our mission was not to win terrain but simply to kill."

But the North Vietnamese fighters, the Vietcong, were difficult to defeat. As the years wore on, more and more U.S. troops died in what seemed a useless, never-ending battle. The antiwar protesters objected to America's intervention in a foreign war; to the huge amount of money being poured into the war effort; and especially to the mounting death toll. In 1973, the United States withdrew all its remaining forces from Vietnam and, in the following year, stopped all military aid to South Vietnam. Without American backing, North Vietnam soon invaded South Vietnam and captured Saigon. South Vietnam's surrender, on April 30, 1975, signaled the first U.S. defeat in war.

Starting that fall, the demonstrations only escalated as students nationwide began to increasingly express their outrage against the war. They also protested civil rights abuses and the U.S. government's handling of a wide range of other issues. By spring 1970, the United States was a cauldron boiling over with antigovernment, antiwar sentiment. Few college campuses remained removed from the furious social upheaval taking place.

Then, on May 4, 1970, the Ohio Army National Guard moved in on war protesters at Kent State University in Kent, Ohio. Beyond belief to most people at the time, they fired on unarmed students. Four were killed and nine wounded. With this shocking act, an explosive wave of violent antiwar demonstrations broke out. Students from around the world reacted to what had occurred at Kent.

Lisa was now far from the insulated world she had lived in during her early teens. As part of the widespread student uprising, she went on strike with the rest of the Princeton student body. Final exams didn't happen. Along with other students, Lisa was even tear-gassed during one demonstration. Queen Noor wrote in her memoir,

 It was a seminal moment in shaping my view of American society. While I loved my country, I found my trust in its institutions badly shaken.

A MINOR DETOUR

After the incident at Kent State, thousands of American students became disillusioned with the educational establishment. Many of them stayed in school only to avoid being drafted into the war. But scores of other students dropped out because they felt their schools were not serving them well. Some just wanted to be fully involved in the anti-establishment movement.

Lisa was one of those who had grown dissatisfied at school. In the winter of her second year, after only three semesters at Princeton, she dropped out. From New Jersey she made her way to the lively ski town of Aspen, Colorado. There she got work as a waitress in a pizza place and had a job for a while as a hotel maid. She also connected with the well-regarded Aspen Institute. This was a nonprofit organization devoted to "enlightened leadership" and to promoting understanding among the world's peoples. At the institute, she worked in the library and on projects that interested her deeply.

These various jobs provided enough money to live on, but Lisa's perfectionist dad was not pleased. Dropping out of any school, let alone Princeton, was something he could barely tolerate. When Jeeb, fuming with anger, flew out to argue his point, his daughter stood her ground. She was committed to taking a year off. Her goal was to discover how resourceful she could be on her own. Jeeb could not change her mind.

The Aspen Institute provided a lively intellectual atmosphere for nineteen-year-old Lisa. Her horizons continued to expand. One event that especially influenced her was a conference called "Technological Change and Social Responsibility." One of the speakers deeply impressed her: Buckminster Fuller, a legendary architect, thinker, and inventor of the geodesic dome. Another of her best experiences at the Aspen Institute was being part of a far sighted architectural project. This further opened her mind to new possibilities.

After her year in Colorado, Lisa returned to Princeton to complete her degree. Now back at school, she drew on the knowledge and experiences she had gained at the Aspen Institute. For instance, she decided to major in architecture and urban planning. Lisa selected a wide range of courses that would prove helpful in her future career. Some of these included art, engineering, and history classes. She also learned practical skills that would benefit her throughout her life. She claims that one of the most important of these skills was "practice in thinking on my feet when faced with merciless critiques of my work."

OUT INTO THE WORLD

Princeton's first coed class graduated in 1973. By this time, women students were an accepted part of campus life. Mutual respect between the sexes had not always been common. Now it was not rare at all. One of Lisa's classmates was S. Georgia Nugent, who later became a Princeton professor. As an adult, Professor Nugent told one journalist that going to Princeton had turned out to be "a tremendous advantage to those of us who went on to professional lives in fields largely dominated by men."

Lisa was certainly one of those women. She graduated in 1974 with a degree in architecture and urban planning. She was entering a field that had long been a male stronghold—but this would not hold her back.

After graduation, Lisa traveled abroad to see what interesting possibilities she could find. She landed in Sydney, Australia, where she hoped to work for a British-based architectural firm that had

A BLANK SLATE

During her years of high school and college, Lisa participated in many student activities. At Chapin she joined the school's tutoring program and helped illiterate students in New York City's Harlem neighborhood learn to read. When she was elected to a class office, however, the school authorities would not let her accept the position. They stated that Lisa was "apathetic and negligent. But she suspected that they actually objected to her independent spirit.

At Concord Lisa played field hockey and skied. And at Princeton she was one of the school's first female cheerleaders. In the 1974 college yearbook, students typically had long lists of accomplishments beside their pictures. But Lisa's extracurricular focus had been social justice, something not usually detailed in a yearbook. No list accompanies her yearbook picture. The white space beside that photo is like a blank slate that nevertheless says a lot.

Lisa Halaby was one of the few Princeton students who did not have a long paragraph of accomplishments beside her yearbook picture.

offices there. Because of work permit problems, she wasn't able to take the job. But after finding a position with another architectural firm, she remained in Australia for the next year.

Lisa's Australian job involved projects being built in the Middle East. Because of her Syrian roots, this work especially interested her. When her job ended, she decided to continue following that interest. Again, the Aspen Institute was helpful. An institute conference in Persepolis drew her attention. Once an important city in ancient Persia, Persepolis is now part of Iran.

WORK IN THE MIDDLE EAST

As luck would have it, at the end of the Aspen Institute conference, Lisa had a meeting with the director of the American branch of Llewelyn-Davies Weeks. This was the architectural and planning firm she had been unable to work for in Australia. She liked the idea of joining them now. The result of the meeting in Persepolis was an offer of a job as an assistant planner for the firm. Lisa accepted.

To Lisa, the best part about this position was that it did not require her to work in the United States. Instead, the project was based in Tehran, the capital of Iran. Buoyantly, she set off for that city in fall 1975. What she found was her dream job. Reza Pahlavi, the shah, or ruler, of Iran, wanted a model city built in north Tehran. It was a massive urban planning project. The shah's vision for this giant new city included everything from tree-lined promenades to sprawling malls to embassy buildings. The architects at Llewelyn-Davies Weeks were going to turn that vision into reality.

As an assistant, Lisa's job was to survey all the structures surrounding the vast building site. After surveying, she drafted maps of these areas. Being female and, at twenty-four, the youngest person on the team might have been intimidating for someone else. But it wasn't for Najeeb Halaby's eldest daughter. Casually dressed and never wearing makeup, she dove right in.

Since she didn't judge others by their physical appearance, Lisa assumed others would treat her the same way. She expected to be evaluated by how well she did her job and the kind of person she was. Nevertheless, she was now in a professional environment. Different standards applied. The men on her team, she has said,

> treated me like a little sister, making brotherly attempts to sophisticate me, encouraging me to use makeup and make more of an effort with my loose, flowing hair.

Tehran, the capital of Iran, is its largest city as well as the country's center of industry.

MODESTY OR SUBMISSION?

As an American woman, Lisa did not dress in a traditionally Middle Eastern fashion. But she was not unique. Urban Iranian women, and those from the country's upper and middle classes, did not dress in this traditional style either. Today, as a Muslim and Jordanian royal, Queen Noor dresses more modestly than is typical in the West. But she has strong views about women being entirely covered. "As religious extremism started to develop," she told a reporter in the early 1990s, "there came a form of dress that was [colorless and] covered the body from neck to toe. Over it is worn a headdress that is restrictive, an uglifying fashion psychologically, to defeminize . . . to make women totally unappealing, to negate their femininity. It is a symbol of submission."

In a more recent magazine interview, Queen Noor explained the headscarf that many Muslim women wear, even without long robes: "Islam calls for men and women to behave and dress modestly. Modest dress for many does not require having to cover up the head. But now, I think, for an increasing number of Arabs and Muslims, there is a resistance to [western women's style of] dress and behavior. It is a way of saying, 'I don't want to be judged by my appearance. I want to be judged by what I am.' For others, it is a way of identifying themselves as Muslims, respecting a more conservative set of personal and social values."

This was not surprising. Tehran was the picture of ancient beauty and exotic scenery. But it was also a dynamic, sophisticated, and modern city. Being immersed in the culture was invigorating for the young Lisa.

Underneath those gossamer *chadors* [body shawls], hip young women wore bellbottom jeans and platform shoes. . . . The treatment of women was nuanced as well. I never felt pressured or intimidated when traveling alone or moving from one place to another, but I was often stared at strangely.

LEAVING TEHRAN

Lisa's life in Tehran was exciting. As well as doing satisfying work, she immersed herself in the culture. She saw incredible wealth as well as extreme poverty. Through family connections, she made friends with several Tehranis from whom she got an inside view. She also became friends with Shah Pahlavi and his wife. She found it encouraging that the shah had given both his wife and his sister important positions of authority in Iran.

I observed these developments with interest," Queen Noor has said. "As a young professional, I was intrigued by the special challenges facing women in their public and private lives, particularly highly visible and active women.

At the same time, the Iranian people were growing more dissatisfied with the shah's rule. Some felt Iran was becoming a police state, as the government cracked down on anyone considered a threat. The brewing impulse for revolution came from two opposing factions of society. One group, which was liberal, pushed for human rights and the greater freedoms that democracy affords. The other side consisted primarily of deeply conservative Shiite Muslims, who wanted the rigid codes of Sharia, or Islamic sacred law, to be reinstated.

As the unrest increased throughout Iran, Llewelyn-Davies Weeks began to feel the heat. At the same time, Lisa's attitude toward the shah's model city started changing. Now she realized that the building of this elaborate project could cause major environmental and social problems.

More important, living in Tehran had impressed on Lisa a greater problem. She clearly saw significant misunderstanding and mistrust between the West and the Middle East. If Americans and other westerners were unable to see all the good she had seen, how would peace ever become a reality? Once again the urge to do something to improve cultural relations was directing her course.

By mid-1976, many people no longer felt safe in Tehran. This was true even within the Llewelyn-Davies firm. But the project Lisa was working on had reached its next phase. The architects began returning to their home base in England to continue their work there. Lisa was the last employee to leave Iran. She did not plan to continue in the field of architecture, however. She had a new goal now. "[F]orging understanding between cultures," she later noted about that time, "seemed even more urgent than urban planning."

CHAPTER FOUR

Connecting with a King

"**Y**OU WILL RETURN TO ARABIA," the fortune-teller predicted. He stared into Lisa's empty coffee cup and studied the leftover grounds for further messages. "And you will marry someone highborn, an aristocrat from the land of your ancestors."

The "fortune-teller" was, in fact, simply one of Lisa's acquaintances. The occasion was a good-bye dinner in Tehran in 1976. Like others working there for Llewelyn-Davies Weeks, Lisa was about to leave Iran. For fun, the man had tried his hand at this old Middle Eastern method of reading the future.

The fortune certainly sounded romantic. But that night it seemed a long stretch from reality. Lisa was planning to return to New York City. Other than that, the only thing she knew for sure about her future was that she expected to change careers. Now her ambition was to become a journalist. She had decided that writing and publishing was a better way for her to contribute to the world.

Within a year, however, Lisa's destiny appeared to be unfolding just as that fortune-teller had predicted. Since 1973, Najeeb Halaby had been working on a variety of important aviation-related projects in Jordan. His Majesty King Hussein of Jordan had hired Jeeb as an aviation consultant. Jeeb also served as

A view of Amman, Jordan's capital city

director of the Jordanian airline's international advisory board. Additionally, he had established an aviation company in Amman, Arab Air Services.

From the time of her parents' 1973 visit there, Lisa had heard much about Jordan and its king. In 1976, she even unexpectedly met him. That winter Jeeb took her with him on a brief trip to Jordan. At the airport in Amman, while attending an important ceremony with her father, Lisa had been introduced to King Hussein and his wife, Queen Alia. At Jeeb's request, Lisa had taken a picture of King Hussein and Jeeb standing together on the tarmac. This photo documented the moment when her life began to take a new direction.

A DATE WITH DESTINY

In the early months of 1977, Lisa returned to Jordan. It was her second trip there since leaving Iran. She had accepted a job working for her father. The position was temporary, lasting less than a year. Once her work was done, she planned to return to the United States and to get on with becoming a journalist.

Before she could leave the country, however, she was offered another interesting opportunity. The head of the Jordanian airline asked Lisa to be in charge of a new department. She would coordinate the planning and design of the airline's worldwide facilities. It was an offer that the challenge-loving American had to accept.

Since meeting King Hussein, Lisa had come in contact with him many times at the airport. But these encounters occurred within the course of the busy business day. They were always friendly but brief.

In spring 1978, however, Jeeb urged Lisa to accompany him to a meeting with the king. The meeting was to be held in the king's offices at the Diwan, the royal court. Lisa resisted. She had not been invited to be part of this royal audience. But in the end she *was* invited. King Hussein himself asked her to join them in his chambers.

At the end of that meeting, the king made another unexpected request of Lisa. Hashimya Palace, his royal residence in Amman, had some construction problems. He wanted Lisa to visit the palace and to give him her architect's opinion on the work being done. She agreed, and they scheduled a lunch date for the very next day. In her journal for that day, April 7, 1978, Lisa marked the event in two brief words. "Hash. 12:30."

By then, the forty-two-year-old king had been a widower for more than a year. His period of mourning was over, so he was Jordan's most eligible bachelor. His courting of Lisa began the next day during that lunch date. Much later he revealed to her that he had first fallen for her the previous day, during the meeting in his offices.

The lunch date lasted long past midday. After their meal, King Hussein gave Lisa a tour of the palace, which had plenty of problems indeed. When he asked her to take charge of the renovations, her reply was not the kind that a king typically hears. But it was absolutely in keeping with her honest, straightforward nature. Lisa let him know that she was not qualified to take on this kind of work. Instead, she offered to help him find people who were.

That honesty impressed King Hussein. Lisa stayed at the palace throughout the rest of the day. She was introduced to the king's three youngest children, and later that day he took her to visit the royal stables, where his family bred some of the world's finest Arabian horses.

QUEEN ALIA AND HUSSEIN'S OTHER WIVES

Only a few months after Lisa's first introduction to the king and queen of Jordan, tragedy struck King Hussein's family. Queen Alia, his third wife, was killed in a helicopter crash in February 1977. She was only twenty-eight years old. This left the king a widower with eight children. The youngest three were Hussein's children with Alia, whom he married in 1972. Queen Alia gave birth to two of the three children, Princess Haya in 1974 and Prince Ali in 1975. Then, in 1976, the royal couple adopted a daughter, Abir, a Palestinian orphan born in 1972.

Queen Alia, who was of Palestinian origin, had an exceptional position, historically unlike any of the other wives of Jordanian kings. She was the first queen of Jordan ever to take on a vital public role alongside the king. Alia had actively developed numerous social and cultural programs in Jordan.

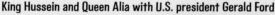

King Hussein and Queen Alia with U.S. president Gerald Ford

Her work had focused especially on helping women and children. One of her greatest causes was making sure children from poor families received a good education. Queen Alia International Airport, built in 1983, was named in her honor.

King Hussein's first marriage was short-lived. In 1955, he wed Sharifa Dina bint Abdul-Hamid, known as Queen Dina. He was just nineteen, and she was twenty-six. Hussein had only been king a short time when he met Dina, a distant cousin from Egypt. In 1956 they had a daughter, Princess Alia. That same year, the couple separated. They divorced the following year. Their daughter, Princess Alia, remained with the king.

In 1961, King Hussein married British-born Antoinette Avril Gardiner. After their marriage and her conversion to Islam, she was given the name Princess Muna. She never received the title of queen. Together, King Hussein and Princess Muna had four children. The first, Abdullah, born in 1962, is now King Abdullah II of Jordan. The others include Prince Faisal (1963) and

Princess Muna with baby Abdullah II

twin daughters Princess Aisha and Princess Zein (1968). King Hussein and Princess Muna divorced in December 1971.

When Lisa returned home that evening, it was behind the steering wheel of one of the king's cars. He had insisted she drive, despite her reluctance and embarrassment. Seated beside her in the passenger seat, he delighted in the mischievous fun of it. A motorcade of security guards accompanied them.

From that point on, the courtship began in earnest. Lisa would tell a journalist several years later,

We courted on a motorcycle. It was the only way we could get off by ourselves. Of course we were always followed.

Those followers were members of King Hussein's security forces. The couple tried to stay out of the public eye. They explored the city and visited the Dead Sea by motorcycle. They took helicopter rides to view Jordan from the air and spent many evenings at home in the palace with the king's children.

Only eighteen days after their fateful lunch date, King Hussein mentioned for the first time his desire to speak with Lisa's father. It was not the last time. And not long afterward, as he was about to embark on a state visit to Yugoslavia, he gave her two gifts. One of them was a gold ring set with a cluster of tiny diamonds.

The clues were adding up. It looked as if Lisa might soon have a major decision to make. She realized, much to her surprise, that the king was intending to propose.

CHAPTER FIVE

Jordan's New Queen

KING HUSSEIN OF JORDAN, HEAD OF A country embroiled in Middle Eastern conflict. A man who had survived numerous assassination attempts, who still faced occasional death threats. The object of constant media attention. Three previous wives and eight children.

If Lisa Halaby had made a list of the pros and cons of marrying Jordan's ruler, these likely would have been a few of the negative points. But there were many positives as well.

The king was kind, intelligent, generous, and empathetic. An optimistic and tireless peacemaker. Forgiving of friends and even enemies. Easier to talk to than any man Lisa had known before. Wealthy, powerful, handsome—and in love with her. And, it turned out, she was in love with him.

In the weeks after King Hussein formally proposed, the pluses and minuses of accepting weighed heavily on Lisa's mind. She loved the Arab world and felt a deep connection to it through her heritage. But she worried that the Jordanian people and the rest of the Middle East would not accept an American as King Hussein's wife. She was concerned that her liberal background would bring on negative publicity. She was nervous about always being in the public spotlight. And how would she handle suddenly being part of such a large family, especially as a brand-new stepmother?

Lisa with King Hussein in Amman, shortly before their wedding in 1978

RULERS OF THE HASHEMITE KINGDOM OF JORDAN

In 1946, the Hashemite Kingdom of Jordan was established as an independent country. Its king, Abdullah I, was King Hussein's grandfather. The Hashemites are considered direct descendents of the Prophet Muhammad, and King Abdullah was a great-grandson of Muhammad.

King Abdullah made great strides in developing the nation before his death. Under his rule, Jordan saw the development of its first constitution. It also had its first parliamentary elections.

But not everyone appreciated the king's progressive impulses. Abdullah was assassinated in a Jerusalem mosque—an Islamic house of worship—in 1951. At issue was the explosive conflict between Israel and Palestine. The assassin, who had accomplices behind the scenes, was a Palestinian carrying out a political act against a man whose moderate views conflicted with those of most Arabs. King Abdullah had not objected to the creation of a Jewish state. Many people distrusted him and his apparent intentions to absorb Palestinian territory into what was then Transjordan. They further suspected that he, along with the leaders of Lebanon, sought a separate peace with Israel.

At the time King Abdullah was assassinated, his beloved fifteen-year-old grandson was standing only a few feet away. After shooting Abdullah in the head, the gunman fired on the king's grandson. The bullet hit a medal pinned to his jacket, which saved the boy's life. It was a medal his grandfather had insisted he wear that day.

That lucky grandson was Hussein bin Talal, the man later officially known as King Hussein of the Hashemite Kingdom of Jordan. The incident in the mosque was only the first of many attempts on his life.

Despite this, King Hussein followed in his grandfather's footsteps. His own father, Talal, was proclaimed king after Abdullah's assassination. He ruled for less than a year, however, because of mental health problems. Hussein was only sixteen when his father stepped down. By Jordanian law, he was not old enough to be the country's ruler, so a regent temporarily took over the governance of the country. Hussein was proclaimed king on May 2, 1953, his eighteenth birthday according to the Arabic calendar.

King Hussein was educated at Victoria College in Alexandria, Egypt, and at Harrow School and the Royal Military Academy, Sandhurst, both in England. He was known for his commitment to bettering the lives of the Jordanian people and for his tireless diplomatic efforts to establish peace in the Middle East.

Toward the end of his life, King Hussein spoke at the Summit of the Peacemakers in Sharm el-Sheikh, Egypt. He spoke out eloquently against terrorism and in support of peace. As he concluded his speech, Hussein expressed his vision for Jordan: "My country will always be on the front line in the effort to protect the peace process and to maintain the gains made by ordinary people. Our commitment to human rights and democratization will remain a constant component of our national identity, and a guiding light for our actions in the Arab, Islamic, and international arenas."

In the end, love led Lisa to her decision. Though she realized there would be many challenges, she joyfully agreed to marry Hussein. They set a date only weeks away—June 15, 1978.

Even before the official announcement, Lisa found herself in a whirlwind of activity—and publicity. In almost a single instant, her life changed forever. Immediately, the hubbub around her was so great that she could not return to her own apartment or office to collect her belongings. Other people brought everything she owned to the house she would live in until the wedding. She could not even fulfill her plans to shop for a wedding dress in Paris because leaving the country was out of the question.

Lisa's carefree days as a single woman—and her days when strangers paid little attention to her—were over. She was now operating under a whole new set of terms.

Before Lisa became involved with King Hussein, she was already studying the Arabic language and Jordanian history. Now she put even greater dedication into those studies. She also began studying the Quran, Islam's sacred text. Her intention was to become a Muslim like her husband-to-be.

Though she came from a Christian tradition, Lisa had not followed any particular religion herself. Nor had she been forced to accept the Islamic religion. Jordan's kings are free to marry anyone who comes from a religion that believes in only one God. Lisa was naturally drawn to adopting King Hussein's religion and found it suited her own beliefs well.

Among Islam's many tenets, or codes of belief, Lisa appreciated its insistence on the equality of rights between men and women. She also liked the Islamic version of the Golden Rule: "Not one of you is a true believer until he desires for his brother what he desires for himself."

Early on the morning of her wedding, Lisa officially accepted the Muslim religion. She became a Sunni Muslim, like the majority of Jordanian Muslims. In the days before that, the king had also given her a new name. She was to be called Noor al Hussein, "the light of Hussein."

Becoming Noor was something the young American welcomed. At the same time, she did not give up her independent spirit or willingness to break with tradition. Typically, in a Muslim marriage, the bride is not present. Only men witness the ceremony, which is a simple signing of a contract. The bride chooses a close male relative to represent her.

Noor, however, refused to be absent from her own wedding rites. On that day, she sat beside King Hussein in the elegant drawing room of his mother's palace. She acted as her own witness to the ceremony, performed by a sheikh, or Muslim religious leader. It was the first time a bride in Jordan's Hashemite line of descendants had ever attended her own wedding ceremony.

The ritual was short and simple. Wearing a white silk dress made especially for her, Noor spoke the traditional Islamic wedding vows. She carried white orchids from Uncle Camile's Colombian farm. The couple sealed their vows in the traditional Muslim way: they clasped right hands rather than exchanging wedding rings.

Meanwhile, a large crowd of journalists and television cameras captured the couple's every move from the other end of the room. Many of them focused on the fact that the new bride was only two months from her twenty-seventh birthday, while the king would be forty-three in November. They also could not stop mentioning the fact that the queen was 2 inches (6 centimeters) taller than the king. As with the American actress Grace Kelly's marriage to King Rainier III of

THE NAMES OF NOOR

Lisa Halaby never truly felt her first name fit her. Her mother originally wanted to name her Camille. This was the name of Najeeb Halaby's uncle, who lived in Colombia, South America. Doris Halaby thought a great deal of Uncle Camile, but he objected to giving his name to the new baby. He felt it was too Arabic for an American girl. He suggested the name Mary Jane. Instead, her parents chose Lisa. But their daughter noted later that she always felt much more like a Camille. Or perhaps a Noor.

Monaco in 1956, the news of this match hit the media worldwide.

Queen Noor's wedding was hardly the type she had envisioned for herself during her student days. She wrote in her memoir,

Like many women of my generation, I always thought I would be married barefoot on a mountaintop or in a field of daisies.

King Hussein and Lisa Halaby at their wedding ceremony in the royal palace

SPEAKING OUT FOR MUSLIM WOMEN

Queen Noor is hardly the only Muslim woman to have challenged traditional Islamic codes of behavior. Like her, many Middle Eastern women have studied the Quran to understand what it says about the role of women. In doing so they have discovered no texts that support many of the current "rules" that seem to dictate what women are allowed to do or not to do. Toujan al-Faisal, the first woman elected to the Jordanian parliament, has been speaking out about these issues—at her own risk—for years. In 1988, she was a television journalist, covering women's affairs in Jordan. "It turned out to be the most controversial series in the history of Jordanian television," she told an American reporter. "Local newspapers received hundreds of letters of protest from outraged men."

But the hate mail and the injustices against women just made Faisal stronger. "[The men] maintained that . . . my program was challenging God's order. . . . I rebutted the fundamentalists within the context of Islam," she said. "I quoted directly from the Quran and the sayings of the Prophet. What these men have created is a distortion, but the fundamentalists said I was a heretic [or nonbeliever] and that I wanted four husbands for myself."

Over time, Queen Noor has become one of the strongest spokespeople in defense of Muslim women's rights. Like Faisal, she outspokenly objects to what she calls the "traditional patriarchal societies which try to keep them [women] in bondage." She also hopes to enlighten people about her religion. In a 2008 magazine interview she said,

Few westerners realize that seventh-century Islam granted women political, economic, legal, and social rights unheard of in the West. These rights were based on the teaching of the equality of men and women before God—and this is when most of the rest of the world considered women chattel [property].

SETTLING IN

After a brief honeymoon in Scotland, King Hussein and his new bride returned to Jordan. Before their marriage, Noor had not given much thought to what her official royal title would be. The king never told her directly. Instead, she found out by watching a TV news report shortly after their wedding day. She was surprised to hear the newscaster announce that Hussein had given her the title of queen.

She was now Queen Noor al Hussein. This prestigious title brought her even greater attention. But she remained focused on the many things she still had to learn about her new role. In some cases, she would have to discover how to strike a balance between acting as people expected her to and being herself. It wasn't always easy. "Sure it was hard for her in the beginning," said a friend from Noor's time at the Cathedral School. "She had no family. No buddies."

Aside from her dedication to King Hussein and her stepchildren, Queen Noor had another important matter to sort out. That was figuring out how she could best contribute to the nation of Jordan. Some members of the royal court quickly told her that her role would be limited to official ceremonial activities. But Noor had a much broader idea of how she could contribute as queen.

Noor had agreed to marry King Hussein with the assurance that she could continue to work and to take an active role in areas that were important to her.

I knew that no matter what happened, I would always have my work and the contributions I could make to the country.

She wrote,

The King had let me know . . . that he was offering me a partnership. . . . I had a job to do for the country I already loved and an extraordinary man as a partner.

It was good to have this assurance as she moved into her own offices at Al-Ma'wa. This was the royal residence Noor had lived in before her marriage. Now it was set up to be a sanctuary for her professional life. She had had to stop working for the airlines the moment her engagement was announced. Now she welcomed the chance to return her attention to productive and stimulating projects.

First she had to determine where to begin. Noor had high ideals concerning what she could do as queen. Looking back she noted, "I wanted the office and the projects that would emanate from it to represent the best of Jordan and reflect the country's rich diversity."

In the months to come, many important projects would begin in Queen Noor's offices at Al-Ma'wa. The new American queen would greatly benefit the nation of Jordan.

CHAPTER SIX

Making a Difference

J ORDAN HAD A NEW QUEEN! THE WHOLE world wanted a glimpse of her. She was young and beautiful, and the public was ready to be dazzled. High-fashion gowns and a glittering tiara were an expected part of the package. But the glamour and glitter associated with a queen did not exactly fit Queen Noor's naturally low-key style. At the time of her engagement she owned only a few simple skirts, shirts, and casual blazers—and a lot of jeans. She rarely wore jewelry, and the pieces she had were far from flashy. She never wore makeup.

Now that she was queen, however, all eyes would be on her whenever she appeared in public. Every magazine and news-paper that reported on Queen Noor invariably mentioned her appearance. This meant a major revamping of her wardrobe. For a young woman who wanted her ideas to matter more than her looks, this was exasperating. She remarked in her memoir,

 It has always puzzled me that a woman in the public eye is judged first for her appearance, then for her achievements.

The royal couple together in Amman in 1979

Noor still had a lingering discomfort with calling attention to herself. She had always felt most at ease wearing simple clothes and hairstyles. Part of her also believed it was inappropriate to indulge in an image of luxury when Jordan had so much poverty.

Nevertheless, out of necessity, she began to adapt. Her husband, for one, liked seeing her in elaborate and bold-colored styles at dressy events. She also had to get used to wearing flashy and expensive jewels at some special occasions. It was not hard for her to enjoy wearing beautiful and elegantly designed fashions from some of the world's top designers.

Queen Noor did her best to find a workable compromise between her natural style and what people expected of her. She did not always feel successful at this, however:

Over the years I tried to achieve a balance between an understated style and the need to look regal but invariably erred, in my view, by going to one extreme or the other.

In her style of dress, Queen Noor had to, as one magazine journalist put it, "bridge the gap between two cultures. After a brief fling with head-to-toe Valentino couture [high fashion design] right after she married, she found herself drawn to the embroidered robes made in her adopted country. Fashionable Jordanians followed her lead. . . .

[This created] a demand that enabled poor women to earn money at home through sewing and embroidery."

Dealing with the constant rumors and gossip was another new difficulty. Rumors about Noor began to blossom even before her wedding. Even more tales swirled through the media once she was queen. As is true of most celebrity stories, the majority were negative and had little basis in fact. Some hurt her feelings or just plain annoyed her. Others were so outrageous that she was shocked anyone would take them seriously. Many of the worst were entirely made-up tabloid newspaper tales. Some reported that Noor spent outrageous sums of money on jewelry and other luxury items. Another claimed she had bought an entire island in Asia.

Due to her unusual marriage, Queen Noor discovered, the rumor mill was not temporary. In a 1996 speech she gave in Washington, D.C., she told listeners,

> [T]he Western media seemed to decide that their audiences . . . were only interested in what I wear, what I eat, and what I do in my leisure time. . . . [T]hey have exaggerated, invented stories, or fallen back upon commercially successful stereotypes of Arabs, Muslims, and women.

The circulation of these untrue or overblown stories would be a fact of Noor's life as long as she remained queen. Eventually, she learned not to take them personally. She found it hard to understand, though, why people were always so ready and eager to believe them.

GETTING STARTED

Queen Noor did not waste much time brooding on false media reports. She had many more important things to think about. At home, she concentrated on how she could contribute to her marriage and to Hussein's already large family. She also had to learn how to act properly in unfamiliar cultural situations.

Noor confessed in an interview a few years after her marriage,

"

There was no time for me to be educated to any of the patterns of life here, the little protocols. I had to pick it up as we were going and there was a great deal of pressure. Sometimes I would say to His Majesty, 'I just don't understand.'

"I was struck by her dignity and her determination to be the best wife and queen," said Sarah Pillsbury, an old friend who saw Noor

about a year after her wedding. "The king never said to her, 'Do this, do that.' She figured it out herself."

In fact, she had to. In the early days of their marriage, Queen Noor had sought King Hussein's advice about where she could do the most good. The king's reply was short and simple. "I have complete faith in you," he said. "You have never made a mistake."

Queen Noor was on her own, but she felt confident. Identifying three areas in which she thought she could make a difference—social issues, culture, and the environment—she plunged in. She had lived in Jordan for quite a while before meeting and marrying King Hussein. This gave her a general understanding of the country's history and culture. It also made her well aware of Jordan's many social problems.

Now Noor had the opportunity to address some of these very real problems and to find ways to solve them. Right away, though, she was in for a surprise. She discovered that some members of the royal court were shocked at the idea of her functioning independently from her husband. These men could not fathom that the queen would make decisions for herself or competently start new ventures on her own.

This hardly held her back. Queen Noor knew many strong, independent Middle Eastern women. She also understood that the men's attitude reflected a widespread cultural belief. This belief was that women did not have the same professional capabilities that men had. Noor's husband, although ruler of a traditionally patriarchal society, did not hold these same beliefs.

Given her husband's support and her professional background and experience, it was not surprising that Queen Noor proved the royal court wrong. She was soon immersed in a wide range of diverse causes. And over time, her adopted homeland began to benefit greatly from the many innovative programs she developed.

Among the queen's contributions was persuading Jordanian public works officials to establish the country's first nationwide building code. She worked hard to increase sustainable tourism in Jordan and to protect the environment. In the early 1980s, Noor helped establish the National Committee for Public Buildings and Architectural Heritage. This organization is in charge of preserving, restoring, and protecting important archeological sites throughout the land. Two of the most significant sites are the historic port at Aqaba and the ruins of Petra.

AID TO CHILDREN

At the time Noor became queen, the Jordanian birthrate was two times higher than the average in other developing nations. More than half the country's population was fifteen years old or less. A full 20 percent were younger than five. Schools were overcrowded and undersupplied. Jordan's medical facilities were overextended, partly due to the country's large refugee population. Severe poverty was an ongoing problem. Understandably, helping children would be one of the queen's first and most important endeavors.

In 1979, Queen Noor became head of Jordan's National Committee for the Child. In this role, she wanted to address health, education, poverty, and other critical social issues. With a group of international organizations and governmental ministers, she began developing numerous child welfare projects.

Within the first year of becoming queen, Noor had already instituted a nationwide vaccine program for children. She also set up literacy programs and made plans to develop urban parks and a children's hospital. Other vital programs she oversaw involved offering more opportunities for girls' education and improving nutrition for

Teacher and students in a simple Jordanian school

all children. Both Queen Noor and King Hussein were most proud of establishing SOS Children's Villages for orphans.

Yet another outstanding child-related program Queen Noor instituted is Jordan's National Music Conservatory (NMC). About NMC she has said,

I felt very strongly that the Conservatory should encourage and offer opportunities for Jordanian children to explore their own musical heritage.

SOS CHILDREN'S VILLAGES

Jordan's SOS Children's Villages project got its start after Queen Noor heard about SOS Kinderdorf International. Austrian prime minister Bruno Kreisky introduced the Kinderdorf program to Noor in the early 1980s. SOS Kinderdorf International had established villages for orphans and abandoned children around the world. The organization began after World War II (1939–1945), when so many children were left alone with no remaining family.

Jordan's partnership in this initiative has been, according to Queen Noor, "long and rewarding. . . . Every SOS Children's Village offers a permanent family-style home to children who have lost their parents or can no longer live with them. Four to ten boys and girls of different ages live together with their SOS mother in a family house, and eight to fifteen SOS Children's Village families form a village community."

Still going strong today, NMC offers music training in Arabic instruments and in classical western styles as well. One of the conservancy's main purposes is to demonstrate "the power of music to promote understanding, peace, and unity across cultural divides." With that aim NMC hosts students from all over the Middle East at its annual summer camp. Queen Noor has said that the NMC, as well as another program she got off the ground—Jordan's Children's Heritage and Science Museum—are two of her favorite cultural initiatives.

In 1990, Noor's contribution to children was widely recognized. That year she represented King Hussein at the United Nations World Summit for Children. Later, at the king's request, her offices established Jordan's National Coalition for Children. The purpose of this organization is to coordinate all Jordanian agencies and programs devoted to children's issues.

Queen Noor has always sought to support more than just the immediate welfare of children.

If young people are ignored and feel disenfranchised, they are at risk to become radicalized. But if they are included in social, economic, and political partnerships, their potential is enormous.

OTHER IMPORTANT ISSUES

As she settled in to being Jordan's queen, Noor's responsibilities as a royal wife increased and her social programs expanded. For the most part, her work did not involve politics. Rather, she saw her role as complementary to her husband's job of ruling the country. She aimed "to fill gaps in our socio-economic policies," she said in a speech in Washington, D.C. This included developing several kinds of cultural programs.

In 1981, Noor inaugurated the first annual Jerash Festival of Culture and Arts. Set in a spectacular location—the ruins of an ancient Roman town known as Jerash—the festival quickly became world renowned. Every year since 2008, the event has brought together musicians and other artists from around the world. Since then, these festivities have merged into a new and larger nationwide event, the Jordan Festival.

Queen Noor also became active in Jordan's Royal Society for the Conservation of Nature (RSCN), which King Hussein founded in 1966. The RSCN was a reflection of the king's forward-looking vision. For many years it remained the only environmental conservation agency in the Middle East.

BANISHMENT OF LAND MINES

A global issue of critical importance to Noor is the effort to ban landmines. These treacherous bomb devices are buried by the thousands throughout many parts of the world. When unsuspecting innocent people set off land mines, they are often maimed, blinded, or killed. Unlike some countries, Jordan has not imported any land mines

QUEEN NOOR'S APPEAL TO PRESIDENT OBAMA

Today, most of the world's countries have signed a document known as the Ottawa Mine Ban Treaty. But the United States, along with China, Iran, Pakistan, North Korea, and Cuba, is not among them. Queen Noor has been trying to get the American government to change this.

In December 2009, Noor wrote an article to mark the twelfth anniversary of the Ottawa Treaty. In that article, titled "Obama's Opportunity to Lead a Landmine-Free World," she reports that since the treaty began, land mine casualties have decreased from 25,000 a year to about 5,000 a year—a reduction of 80 percent. In addition, thousands of stockpiled mines around the globe have been destroyed.

At the end of her powerful appeal, Queen Noor writes, "Just as President Woodrow Wilson, another Nobel laureate, decided to forever ban the use of poison gas in 1925, perhaps President Obama, as he heads to Oslo to accept his Nobel Prize for Peace, will commit the U.S. to join the global movement to ban landmines. I can think of no greater gift to future generations."

since 1974, and Noor is an active spokesperson for removing them from wherever they are found.

These weapons have proliferated into a source of random terror that respects neither time nor territory, and does not distinguish between hostile combatants and schoolboys playing football.

In 1997, following in the footsteps of the late princess Diana of Britain, Noor became a patron of the Landmine Survivors Network. Today she also sits on the advisory board of the International Campaign to Ban Landmines (ICBL).

AN UMBRELLA ORGANIZATION

By 1985, Queen Noor's various social and economic programs were so numerous that they needed a common home, an "umbrella" under which they could all operate. Thus, by royal decree, the Noor Al Hussein Foundation (NHF) was born in September of that year. The foundation focused first on projects to reduce poverty. Queen Noor relates in her memoir,

The meaning of the name, Light of Hussein, reflected our mission to help realize the King's vision for our people, to provide greater opportunity and hope.

Queen Noor outside the royal palace in Amman around 1985

THE NOOR AL HUSSEIN FOUNDATION

Today, the Noor Al Hussein Foundation is active in a wide variety of areas. Its stated mission is "to facilitate lasting change in underprivileged communities by creating economic opportunities, building capacity for self-reliance, and improving livelihoods."

"The NHF focuses on equal opportunity in education and culture, women and children's health and welfare," Queen Noor explains. In her opinion, combining modern methods with a respect for the traditions and heritage of the people involved leads naturally to advancement.

"This integrated approach, I believe, is the only way to achieve sustainable development," says Noor. "Strengthened by increased self-reliance and confidence in themselves, local communities are enjoying a measurable improvement in the quality of life . . . and will be . . . more able to participate in the peace-building process in the era of peace."

From the beginning of their marriage, King Hussein and Queen Noor shared the desire to provide opportunity and hope to their people. They also wanted nothing more than to see peace throughout their region. In the poverty-stricken, conflict-ridden Middle East, Queen Noor's wide-reaching work has contributed greatly to meeting those goals.

CHAPTER SEVEN

Conflict in the Middle East

T HE DRUMS OF WAR HAD BEEN BEATING in the Middle East for many decades when Noor moved to Jordan and became queen. As early as 1916, the British government pledged to support an Arab fight for independence from the powerful Ottoman Empire. It was to Britain's advantage to back the Arabs in this goal. They were in the midst of World War I (1914-1918) and wanted to dethrone the Ottomans as well. The understanding was that, with victory, the Arab countries would unite and take charge of their own lands.

King Hussein's great-grandfather, a powerful Hashemite, led the Great Arab Revolt (1916-1918), the uprising that toppled the Ottoman Empire. The Arab countries that had been under the control of the Ottomans looked forward to their united independence. In the end, however, Britain broke its promises to the Arab forces. Instead of allowing the Arab countries to take control of their lands, Britain followed other plans.

In an agreement with France, Britain claimed the territory that included today's nations of Iraq, Palestine, and Jordan. The agreement gave control of Syria and Lebanon to the French. The division of the former Ottoman Empire did not take into account the welfare of the people living in these regions. But it was not just a disastrously uninformed decision. It was also a complete betrayal of the Arabs who had fought to help the Europeans drive the Ottomans out of power. Inevitably, troubles in the Middle East continued to mount.

Residents of Baghdad, Iraq, watch as British soldiers march through one of the city's main streets in 1917, during World War I.

PALESTINE DIVIDED

In 1917, the British government made another momentous decision: to give Palestinian land, in which Arabs had been living for thousands of years, to Jewish settlers. Known as the Balfour Declaration, this move marked the beginning of the ongoing, modern-day Arab-Israeli conflict.

Thirty years later, in 1947, this life-changing decision became official. In that year the United Nations passed Resolution 181. This measure officially divided Palestine into two separate countries—Palestine and Israel. The terms of the resolution made matters even worse. The Jewish people accounted for only a third of Palestine's population, and they owned only 6 percent of the land. Yet they were awarded 55 percent of that land for the creation of Israel. This decision sparked outrage and resentment among both Muslims and non-Muslims throughout Palestine and the Arab countries.

A UNIQUE PERSPECTIVE

In her memoir Queen Noor wrote in detail about this painful conflict. As a westerner witnessing the problems from inside an Arab nation, she had a unique perspective. Like many other Muslims, she sympathized with the plight of the Jewish people. She understood their deep desire for a homeland, especially after Nazi Germany's attempts to exterminate them during World War II. But, she has admitted, she was disturbed by the way in which "Arabs were cast as the aggressors in the dispute between Israel and the Arab countries, when it was their land that had been seized to resolve a European political problem."

EFFECTS OF THE BALFOUR DECLARATION

Until the Balfour Declaration, Muslims, Jews, and Christians had lived relatively peacefully together in the Israel-Palestine region for hundreds of years. This decision disrupted that peace. The declaration held two seemingly contradictory messages. First, it called for "the establishment in Palestine of a national home for the Jewish people." But in the next section it stated that "nothing shall be done that may prejudice the civil and religious rights of existing non-Jewish communities in Palestine."

These two aims were hardly compatible. Jewish Zionists—people who had a strong nationalistic motivation to establish a homeland in the Middle East—began arriving from many other parts of the world to settle in already-occupied territory. They felt the Balfour Declaration entitled them to do so. Inevitably, this influx of settlers disrupted the non-Jewish communities mentioned in the declaration. People were uprooted and pushed out of the land they had lived on for thousands of years. This created a major refugee problem and resulted in mounting resentments and hostilities as the years went on.

Both sides were guilty of terrible acts of violence, but the Israeli forces had the superior power. By the end of 1948, they had taken control of 78 percent of land that was supposed to belong to the Palestinian Arabs. Thousands of Palestinian refugees were streaming into surrounding nations. Transjordan absorbed Palestinian land, as well as a huge portion of these displaced people.

Queen Noor writes,

When I was growing up in the United States, the prevailing view . . . was that Israel was forced to defend itself against hordes of bloodthirsty Arabs pouring across its borders. But now that I was living in Jordan I was discovering that . . . Israel had been on the offensive, demonstrated by the fact that most of the fighting was . . . in the territory [belonging] to the Palestinians.

Like his wife, King Hussein was a humanitarian by nature. And unlike the leaders of many other countries in the region, he opened Jordan to the thousands of people fleeing Palestine. The extreme social and economic pressures this caused in his country weighed on him. But he was also deeply affected by the suffering of these now-homeless masses.

As Queen Noor put it,

This tragic history suffused every aspect of King Hussein's life. For him, matters of state were also matters of the heart.

At the king's side, Noor looked for ways she could also help lessen the suffering.

THE PALESTINIAN LIBERATION ORGANIZATION

Not all the Palestinian refugees remained nonviolent. In 1964, the newly formed Palestine Liberation Organization (PLO) began to fight back against the Israeli forces. With so many displaced and dissatisfied young Palestinians living outside their homeland, PLO membership quickly grew. Although PLO members considered themselves "freedom fighters," some countries—especially Israel and the United States—viewed them as terrorists because of their violent tactics.

By the late 1960s, so many Palestinians lived in Jordan that the PLO considered King Hussein's country its home base in its fight against Israel. Time and again, Jordan suffered major losses when Israelis retaliated against the PLO. In September 1970, some of the most radical members of the PLO hijacked four planes from foreign countries. They landed three of them at a Jordanian airfield and later blew them all up.

THE SIX-DAY WAR

In 1965, as the number of radical Palestinian guerrilla groups rose, conflicts along the Israeli border began to escalate to an intense degree. Although they had the backing of Egypt and Syria, the guerrillas were encouraged to make their attacks from Jordan and Lebanon. The Israelis retaliated, and the violence continued to escalate.

By the end of May 1967, people in the region feared war was imminent. Israel struck first. On June 5, 1967, Israelis made a preemptive attack on Egypt and wiped out nearly all of its air force. As the conflict quickly spread to other Arab states, the Israelis kept control of the skies. Jordan's army moved to defend Arab East Jerusalem, but they were outnumbered and more poorly armed. The Jordanians were soon driven back.

On June 11, 1967, the United Nations ordered a cease-fire in the conflict now known as the Six-Day War or, to the Arabs, *an-Naksah* ("the Setback"). By then, Israel had seized a huge amount of Arab land, including the West Bank, the Gaza Strip, and Arab East Jerusalem. These areas comprised what had remained of Arab Palestine.

Jordan took the hardest hit in this conflict. The nation gained another 300,000 Palestinian refugees, lost 70 percent of its agricultural land, and lost half its industrial establishments. Altogether the war reduced Jordan's gross national product by about 38 percent.

This act of violence was a last straw for King Hussein. But as a national leader, he was in a nearly impossible situation. If Hussein let the PLO continue to operate from Jordan, he would soon lose control of the government and his nation would be destroyed. But if he moved against the PLO, the other Arab states would consider him an ally, or even a puppet, of the West.

As always, the safety, security, and stability of his country were King Hussein's first priorities. That same September, he ordered the Jordanian military to strike against the PLO and attempt to drive them out of the country. A bloody three-week battle followed. The fighting continued for several months, but by summer 1971, the PLO power base had left Jordan and reestablished itself in Lebanon.

Over the following decades, one bitter conflict after another erupted in the Middle East as Israel and the Arab states vied for power and control of land. King Hussein tried to be a mediator and peacemaker, but his attempts at bringing about reasonable negotiations often backfired. At times, both western leaders and heads of Arab states misunderstood his intentions and demonized him. Noor supported her husband's efforts and kept her attention on areas where she could be of service.

REFUGEE SUFFERING

Over the years, Queen Noor increasingly focused on the plight of refugees throughout the world. Aware that life was extremely harsh for displaced people who now lived in Jordan, she began visiting the country's overcrowded refugee camps. She wanted to see the living conditions for herself and to make sure the needs for food, water, and doctors' services were being met. She sometimes took reporters from the West along on these excursions in hopes of bringing broader attention to the refugee situation in the Middle East.

The Noor Al Hussein Foundation has also focused on helping refugees. This became especially true after 2003, when the United States invaded Iraq. After the Iraq War began, hundreds of thousands of refugees fled Iraq for neighboring countries, including Jordan. Noor found the situation heartbreaking. In a 2008 magazine interview, she pointed out that the majority of the refugees "are young women and children, and they face extraordinary challenges from the trauma they've endured in the war. The Noor Al Hussein Foundation . . . is providing medical care, counseling, and pediatric services, with help from international aid groups—but the problem is overwhelming."

Queen Noor visiting a Jordanian refugee camp in August 1990, during the Iraqi invasion of Kuwait

A WITNESS REMEMBERS

One American journalist who accompanied Queen Noor to refugee camps in Jordan later wrote, "Noor jumped in behind the wheel [of the jeep] . . . and we barreled off across the trackless desert. . . . [In] a tent serving as a maternity hospital . . . she inquired whether there was enough food and enough water for showering, and promised to search for more blankets, since the nights had begun to turn cold. After about twenty minutes, she climbed back into the Land Rover, and we drove to another part of the camp, where she repeated this routine."

The NHF provides schooling for Jordan's refugee children and helps their mothers establish their own businesses. It also teaches young people how to use computer technology. Noor believes this "can help [children] avoid becoming absolutely marginalized and hopeless. The kids who benefit from this, and from counseling, are less likely to revert to violence."

SPEAKING IN PUBLIC

Another way in which Queen Noor brought attention to Middle Eastern issues was through public speaking. One of her biggest concerns was what she saw as the West's deep misunderstanding of Arab points of view. In late 1981, Noor accepted an invitation to speak at the Center for Contemporary Arab Studies at Georgetown University in Washington, D.C.

With her husband's agreement, Noor decided to address the pressing political issues of the day rather than stereotypically female-oriented topics. Poised and passionate, she spoke eloquently of her hopes for reconciliation and peace between the West and the Middle East. She stated that "any solution to Arab-Israeli conflict would have to be based on self-determination for the Palestinians, on respect for international law, and on repatriation or compensation for Palestinian refugees."

Standing before five hundred guests, Queen Noor seemed far removed from the extremely shy young girl she once had been. Although her words were impressive, not everyone was pleased with— or interested in—the content of her speech. A *Washington Post* story about the event put great attention on what the queen was wearing.

In her memoir, Noor assesses the response to her speech at Georgetown:

It would be highly controversial in some circles for the wife of a head of state, especially an Arab state, to deliver a political address rather than focusing on more traditional subjects such as children or culture. Hussein would even be accused of using me, but I was no puppet. He and I shared the same frustrations and the same longing for peace and stability in the region.

By early in the new millennium, Queen Noor had become an accomplished and sought-after speaker. She had a clear, humanitarian message that incorporated all she stood for. This message included four major points: breaking down racial stereotypes; meeting the critical needs of the "have-nots" of the world; building worldwide security based on respect for the individual rather than on amassing weapons; and educating and empowering women and youth everywhere.

In a speech in Washington, D.C., in May 2004, Queen Noor summed up her goal as a humanitarian:

> **As an American by birth who chose to embrace my Arab family heritage, I have drawn on my dual perspective to try to replace prejudice and fear with mutual understanding. My long-standing goal has been to create broad-based peace-building coalitions among cultures. . . .**
> **Security has always been a highly charged issue in our region [and the world], and how to achieve it is the subject of endless debate. From my experience, I firmly believe that we need to develop a fundamentally new concept of security, defined not in military but in human terms.**

CHAPTER EIGHT

Balancing Public and Private Life

F OR KING HUSSEIN, RUNNING A COUNTRY was a round-the-clock job. He had long been making valiant efforts to achieve peace among the Middle Eastern nations. Having an intelligent, informed wife who was equally committed to that goal was a great asset. Now the king had a partner who supported him, understood his frustrations, and shared his idealistic vision. Together they focused on what could be done for Jordan and the greater world beyond its borders. But the queen also faced the challenge of managing Hussein's large, active family.

Finding herself a young stepmother to eight children took a lot of adjustment for Noor. At the time Lisa Halaby became queen, King Hussein's children ranged in age from three to twenty-two. Some of them were away at school, but several of the younger ones still lived at home. The new queen had her hands full!

EXPANDING THE FAMILY

Before their marriage, Queen Noor and King Hussein had never discussed the topic of having more children. But early on it became clear that the king was thinking about it. One day, as Noor was drawing up plans for the family's new home, Hussein

The king and queen pose together at home, in about 1980. Queen Elizabeth II of England appears in the photo on the table behind the royal couple.

instructed her to add to the floor plan. He requested she include several extra bedrooms "for the children." He indicated more bedrooms than there were children. Noor realized he was referring to their future children.

The next year, in 1979, the king and queen discovered they were expecting their first child. King Hussein, Noor says in her memoir, was, "in his own words, 'over the moon.'" When Noor and Hussein shared the news with the children, they were excited, too. But sadly, there was to be no new baby. In the fifth month of her pregnancy, while on a visit to England, Queen Noor had a miscarriage. But she and King Hussein could not grieve this loss privately. The story became front-page news in tabloid papers everywhere.

Noor tried to put the experience behind her and, as usual, tried to ignore the public gossip about her family. Doing so was challenging. But about six months later, she learned she was pregnant again. This time the queen took it easy for the first few months before resuming her busy work schedule.

On March 29, 1980, Queen Noor gave birth to a son, the first of her four children with King Hussein. They named him Hamzah. She wrote after his birth,

I had never thought of myself as an especially maternal person, and I was stunned by the intensity of my feelings of love for my firstborn child.

Queen Noor with her four children (*left to right*), Hamzah, Raiyah,
Iman, and Hashim

The second of the king and queen's children, Prince Hashim, was born on June 10, 1981. Their two daughters, Princess Iman and Princess Raiyah, were born on April 24, 1983, and February 9, 1986, respectively.

A FLUENT, HANDS-ON MOM

Even before her own children were born, Queen Noor was as much of a hands-on mom as possible. She had the help of a trained nanny but made the effort to stay deeply involved in the children's lives herself. For example, she became more fluent in her new language, Arabic. She recalls,

> My favorite study moments involved helping my stepchildren with their Arabic homework, which was an unexpected treat. . . .
> [The children] would cuddle up on my bed with me at the end of the day and we would read their first Arabic textbooks together.

Dedicated to learning the language, Noor read Arabic newspapers and lessons from the Quran. She also studied Arabic poetry and worked with a tutor. Eventually she became accomplished enough in her new language to feel comfortable giving public speeches. But mastering Arabic, she confesses in her memoir,

was a long, difficult process that always left me with a raw feeling of inadequacy.

Despite her struggles, Queen Noor had a strong desire to keep improving. This motivation had an added benefit for her sons and daughters. Hussein's first eight children had become fluent first in English. Like Noor, they found it hard to learn Arabic, a more difficult language than English. Recognizing this, the queen began speaking to Hamzah primarily in Arabic from the day he was born. Soon, King Hussein was also using both Arabic and English when he talked to his son. The couple carried on this tradition with the rest of their children, so that they effortlessly mastered both Arabic and English.

WORKING MOTHER

Considering all her responsibilities as King Hussein's wife, Queen Noor was fortunate to have the help of nannies. Before long, she had many national and international projects that needed her attention. One of her proudest achievements happened even before Hamzah was born. In 1979, she established Jordan's Royal Endowment for Culture and Education. A chief aim of the endowment was to award academic scholarships to students pursuing careers in areas most important to Jordan's development. Because of Noor's growing interest in supporting women, the scholarship program also gave special attention to deserving female students.

There were numerous official state events to attend to as well. Early in her marriage, Queen Noor had some of her first experiences as a royal hostess to leaders from neighboring countries. In 1979,

QADDAFI'S FEMALE SOLDIERS

While Queen Noor was pregnant with Prince Hamzah, she and King Hussein had a visit from Colonel Muammar Qaddafi, ruler of Libya. Noor was amused to see that Qaddafi's security forces were all wearing the same "safari suits" their leader was attired in. They all had the same black, curly haircut as well. Jordanian citizens were more fascinated by something else, however. Qaddafi's security forces included women, while Jordan had no active female members in its military. At the time, Queen Noor reported, "I was advocating their inclusion and considered as a model the Women's Royal Army Corps in Britain, which I had visited." As it turns out, perhaps in part through Queen Noor's and King Hussein's influence, the first Jordanian women to undergo military training were in the royal family. In spring 1987, King Hussein's daughter Aisha and two of her female cousins completed the officers' training program at England's prestigious Royal Military Academy, Sandhurst. Princess Aisha's father graduated from the same school.

these included Iraq's then-president, Saddam Hussein, and Libya's longtime leader, Colonel Muammar Qaddafi.

Some months after Hamzah's birth, the queen launched yet another impressive humanitarian program. Her inspiration was the ongoing enmity among the Middle Eastern nations. "If ancient enmities and modern slights continued to divide the Arab world," she realized, there would be little chance for a lasting peace. "Perhaps we could lay the groundwork for more effective cooperation . . . in the future if we began with Arab boys and girls at an early age and brought them together to appreciate their common bonds." From these ideas Noor organized the first annual Arab Children's Congress.

Queen Noor also spent a lot of time driving from one Jordanian village to another. There were many reasons for this. A few of these included setting up and monitoring her vaccine programs, attending urban planning meetings, and, as always, checking on refugee camps. Insisting on being her own driver, Noor savored the few moments she had to get away on her own. She was completely by herself—except for the security vehicle that always followed her.

She remembers,

My private space became the Jeep, and there I would turn up the music, listening to Fairouz, Bach and Beethoven, Bruce Springsteen, and Fleetwood Mac, singing and probably even talking to myself.

TRYING FOR PEACE

While the king and queen's family was growing, the world beyond their royal palace was in continual upheaval. For King Hussein, bringing political stability to the region was crucial. In the early months of Queen Noor's marriage, he had been working hard to organize an international peace conference. His aim was to bring together the countries of Jordan, Palestine, Egypt, and Syria. He wanted all these Arab nations to negotiate collectively with Israel. King Hussein had high hopes that together they could come to a reasonable peace agreement.

Before he had a chance to complete this mission, however, Egypt's president, Anwar Sadat, acted independently. Invited to the United States by then-president Jimmy Carter, Sadat worked out a peace agreement with Israel there. Known as the Camp David Accords, this separate peace outraged the Muslim leaders in Jordan's surrounding countries and shocked King Hussein.

Despite his efforts toward peace, Hussein had not been invited to this gathering with the U.S. president. According to Queen Noor, this was because her husband's insistence that Israel withdraw from all occupied Palestinian territory would have complicated the process of reaching a peace agreement. King Hussein's anticipated peace conference, representing many Arab states, was not to be. He was defeated for the moment, but neither he nor Queen Noor was willing to give up.

ONGOING REGIONAL VIOLENCE

The Arab-Israeli situation was hardly the only conflict Jordan's royal couple had to worry about. In 1980, a bloody war broke out between Iran and Iraq. The reasons for the war were historical and complex.

Queen Noor and the wives of other Middle Eastern leaders meet with first lady Hillary Clinton in the White House in 1995, during the struggle for peace between Israel and Palestine.

It began when Iraq's president, Saddam Hussein, invaded Iran. Iran's shah, or ruling king, had been overthrown the previous year during a violent revolution. Now a radical new Islamic government was in charge. Many political analysts believe one of the main reasons Saddam Hussein invaded Iran was that he feared Iran's powerful new government might spread its extremist influence into Iraq.

Whatever the reasons, the Iran-Iraq War was a grave worry for Jordan's king. Because Jordan shares part of its border with Iraq, King Hussein worried that the conflict might spill over into his country. This never occurred, but the war continued for eight long years. Thousands of lives were lost, and the war did great economic damage to both countries. It also kept Jordan's king on constant alert and feeling the pressure from opposing political forces, both Middle Eastern and western.

Although the Iran-Iraq War finally ended in 1988, Iraq was still bent on war. In 1990, its military invaded the country of Kuwait. The bases of this aggressive move were disputes over oil rights and territorial claims. Although Iraq had long considered Kuwait to be part of its territory, it became indebted to Kuwait during the war. Now Kuwait was allegedly slant drilling Iraqi oil. This was driving the price of oil down, which further harmed the Iraqi economy.

Before the invasion, with trouble brewing, King Hussein had been attempting to broker peace between the two nations. But before he could see the results of his efforts, the situation worsened. Other Arab countries and their western allies intensified and complicated the matter. Iraqi forces charged into Kuwait. This caused thousands more Palestinian refugees to flood into Jordan, this time from Kuwait, where they had established themselves and prospered. It also resulted in a massive, U.S.-led military effort against Iraq.

"This undercutting of King Hussein's mission to achieve an Iraqi commitment on withdrawal," Queen Noor writes in her memoir, "would bring western troops into the region and sow the seeds of radical Islamist terrorist attacks on the United States more than a decade later." Now known as the Persian Gulf War, the conflict lasted from August 2, 1990, through February 28, 1991.

At one point during the Gulf War, the king and queen hosted a dinner for reporters. King Hussein talked about the part he had played in trying to make peace after the Iraqi invasion of Kuwait. "In the first forty-eight hours," one journalist wrote, King Hussein "had gone off to mediate at the request of President [George H. W.] Bush, President Mubarak [of Egypt], and King Fahd [of Saudi Arabia]. . . .

THE QUEEN'S THRONE

While the Gulf War was still raging, an American journalist visited the home of King Hussein and Queen Noor. "If war comes [to Jordan]," he asked the queen, "do you fear losing your throne?"

Noor replied, "In the first place, I don't consider myself as having a throne. The only thing I would ever fear is if the peace and stability that the monarchy has offered to this country were destroyed, if all my husband struggled for, and what I have struggled for by his side, were lost. . . . My happiness, satisfaction, and security do not come from the throne or the monarchy or having been privileged to carry the title of queen of Jordan. . . . Whatever happens, we shall follow King Hussein. For thirty-eight years, his humanity, experience, and wisdom have been what the people identify with."

His efforts at peacekeeping, however, had been misunderstood, mistrusted, or rebuffed by former allies and friends."

Queen Noor agreed. She said, "My husband . . . clearly opposed the Iraqi occupation of Kuwait and . . . was stunned when his . . . efforts to negotiate a peaceful solution were misconstrued by the United States and Britain." These countries had portrayed King Hussein's attempts at peacemaking as an approval of the Iraqi invasion of Kuwait.

"This distortion would be used viciously against King Hussein for years to come," Queen Noor concluded.

TENSION TAKES ITS TOLL

This ongoing state of unrest and misunderstanding wore on King Hussein and Queen Noor. As Noor expressed it, "Jordan, a small country surrounded by volatile neighbors, was always in the middle." Living in a state of tension was a daily experience for Jordan's royal couple. Rumors of attempts on the king's life caused Queen Noor much worry as well. During summer 1991, Noor wrote in her memoir, "our intelligence service and that of the United States were reporting a sharp increase in the number of death threats against King Hussein."

Although the king himself did not fear for his life, the intensity of the political situation took its toll both mentally and physically. He was not sleeping well, and he had occasional episodes of arrhythmia, or irregular heartbeats. Nevertheless, he and Queen Noor did their best to keep their children sheltered from the country's political problems. They scheduled outings to the Red Sea to water ski and fish, took the family on scenic helicopter rides, and made special plans for birthdays and other important occasions. But the king and queen had little time to relax and simply enjoy their life together.

In 1992, King Hussein had another scare. This time, however, it had nothing to do with the region's conflicts. Medical tests detected some precancerous cells in his ureter, the tube that leads from the kidney to the bladder. Doctors successfully removed the cells, and as a safety measure they also decided to remove his kidney.

MOMENTS OF ENJOYMENT

In between King Hussein's treatments, when he was feeling up to it, the couple went on many pleasant excursions in the United States. They spent time with Noor's Washington, D.C.-based family. They also spent an evening in the White House having a dinner of hamburgers with then-president Bill Clinton and first lady Hillary Rodham Clinton.

While the king was receiving treatment in the hospital, Queen Noor frequently visited the children's ward. For fun on Halloween, she dressed the part. "I found a large, elaborate Spanish hair comb with gold filigree and turquoise, shaped like a tiara," she reports, "and I wore a long flowing kaftan." This delighted the children, especially when they saw the nurse who accompanied Noor. Wrapped in strips of bandages, she announced herself as the queen's mummy.

The king recovered and went back to work. But in 1998, he and Queen Noor received much worse news. Not long after a joyous, family-oriented celebration of the couple's twentieth wedding anniversary, Hussein was diagnosed with non-Hodgkin's lymphoma, a type of cancer. Hussein underwent many harrowing months of treatment, overseen by doctors at the renowned Mayo Clinic in Minnesota. All the while Queen Noor was faithfully at King Hussein's side.

"Throughout this time," Queen Noor wrote, "my husband's optimism never lagged. . . . For all the agonies of those months, Hussein and I treasured every moment walking, talking . . . and taking in the small joys of life."

In January 1999, after five and a half months at the Mayo Clinic, King Hussein's doctors told him he was doing well. His cancer was in remission, they said, and he could return home to Jordan.

King Hussein and his family arrived home in the third week of January, during a freezing downpour. Despite the weather, the king insisted on greeting the throngs of Jordanians who lined the street. As the royal motorcade moved slowly along, he stood in the open sunroof of his car.

After his long ordeal, King Hussein was weak and frail. And within days, his health was failing again. Despite urgent efforts on the part of the doctors and a decision to return to the Mayo Clinic, Hussein's condition worsened. When doctors could do no more for him, he was flown back to Jordan with his family. King Hussein died at midday in Amman on February 7, 1999. He was surrounded by Queen Noor and their children.

Noor recalls,

 When Hussein's heart stopped, the heavens literally opened up for an unstoppable rain.

Now his eldest son, Crown Prince Abdullah, would take on the responsibility of being Jordan's king. Queen Noor "turned to Abdullah and said, 'The King has died; long live the King,' and gave him a hug."

King Hussein's funeral was attended by heads of state from around the world. This confirmed the international community's high regard for him. But Queen Noor's presence there outraged some who believed it was unacceptable behavior for a woman.

Independent but well aware of the Muslim codes of behavior, the queen thought differently. "Press accounts at the time said that I was not allowed under Muslim law to attend his funeral, but this simply was not the case," Queen Noor points out. "I knew that I should be with him until he was laid to rest, and that this would in

Queen Noor and her two daughters during King Hussein's funeral at Zahran Palace in Amman, Jordan, February 8, 1999

WHO WOULD BE KING?

Shortly before his death, King Hussein had one important business matter to attend to. He had to decide who would follow him as king of Jordan. For the prior thirty-four years, the king's brother Hassan had been crown prince—the person next in line to rule. But in a controversial move, King Hussein issued a public letter stating that he was changing that decree. He appointed his firstborn son, Abdullah, to be the next crown prince.

The drama of this move had the whole world talking. Abdullah may have been more surprised than anyone. He confessed to Queen Noor that he had never expected to be in line for the throne. He had assumed that role would go to his stepmother's eldest son, Hamzah. Many people outside the royal family believed Queen Noor had unsuccessfully pressured Hussein to make Hamzah king. Noor found these claims ridiculous and strongly supported King Hussein's wishes, whatever they would be. After Abdullah took the throne, he appointed Hamzah crown prince. But a few years earlier Abdullah and his wife, Queen Rania, had their first son. That son, Hussein, was named crown prince in 2009 and is destined to be the next king of Jordan.

no way contradict the teachings of our faith. Societal tradition did not concern me . . . and I will always be grateful to [my advisers] and our Imam, Sheikh Hllayel, for their understanding at such a difficult time."

After King Hussein's death, Queen Noor vowed to follow her husband's example as she continued to work for world peace. Speaking of him, she wrote, "His humanity, his constancy, his decency in a world of deceit and self-interest—all these are unparalleled. . . . I will try to bring my husband's spirit of optimism and moral conviction to everything I do. He never gave up, nor shall I."

Queen Noor has not gone back on that promise. Since her husband's death she has worked tirelessly to improve life for thousands of people around the globe.

CHAPTER nine

Continuing
Contributions

NOT EVERY CHILD GROWS UP IN A FAMILY that teaches the importance of making a contribution to society. But even as a young girl named Lisa Halaby, Queen Noor had been getting this message. As she matured, her social conscience grew, too. Because of her upbringing and her character, she naturally looked for ways she could help improve the world.

Noor's life took her unexpectedly from being a war protester in college to a leader who could make real, on-the-ground differences in the lives of war refugees and others. Becoming queen gave her the opportunities to improve the human condition that she had sought nearly her whole life. She took full advantage of these opportunities throughout her reign. And, inspired by her husband's example, she continues to create new opportunities even today.

In addition to recognition for her work for the Noor Al Hussein Foundation and the King Hussein Foundation, Queen Noor herself has received numerous prestigious honors, awards, and honorary degrees. She is involved in so many organizations, causes, and initiatives to help humanity that to say she is an exceptional humanitarian would be an understatement. These days she focuses her efforts on two areas: empowering women and breaking down what she sees as widespread negative stereotyping of Arabs and Muslims.

Queen Noor is awarded an honorary doctorate degree from Brown University in Providence, Rhode Island, during commencement ceremonies held May 31, 1999.

THE KING HUSSEIN FOUNDATION

King Hussein's legacy endures. Shortly after his death, by royal decree of King Abdullah II, the King Hussein Foundation (KHF) was established. KHF means a great deal to Queen Noor because it commemorates Hussein's lifelong commitment to bettering the world and finding global peace.

The foundation's mission is "to build upon King Hussein's lifelong commitment to peace, sustainable community development, and cross-cultural understanding." This mission is carried out through "national and regional programs that promote education and leadership, economic empowerment, and participatory decision-making."

EMPOWERING WOMEN

One of Queen Noor's most passionate missions is to empower disadvantaged peoples, especially women, in developing nations. As she matured, women's issues became increasingly important to her. But her real awakening to the problems of gender inequality happened only after she had moved out of the United States and was living in the Middle East.

"It really happened on the ground in the developing world," Noor told a reporter about her growing desire to help women. "I began to . . . recognize the importance of [working to change] patterns that restrain women from realizing their potential."

With that in mind, Noor first turned her attention to helping Jordan's rural and impoverished women get their own businesses off the ground. Many of these new businesses reflected the nation's rich culture. The Bani Hamida Women's Weaving Project was one among many highly successful examples. In this venture, female villagers became skilled at creating beautiful hand-dyed rugs. The rugs gave them a steady income and more respected roles within their communities. The work also taught them practical business management skills. Another program that became part of NHF was Noor's National Handicrafts Development program, which included the Bani Hamida project and several others.

Other female-owned businesses, run similarly, produced ceramics, traditional textiles, and other items. These wares not only provided financial stability, but also showed off the talents of Jordan's skilled artisans. The ability to create their own incomes and to function successfully in business gave women hope and a stronger sense of their own worth.

"I began to realize," Queen Noor said about the contrast between the Middle East and the West, "that the vast majority of people in our global family do not grow up as I did in the United States. I had the luxury of feeling that almost anything was possible if you worked hard for it. For so many people, even optimism is a luxury—let alone the ability to plan ahead. . . . [W]e need to listen to people in other cultures and circumstances in order to understand what they are really saying, hoping, and dreaming about."

Queen's Noor's efforts in helping village women establish self-sufficient businesses are well known. Her great successes with these programs have brought her global attention since early in her marriage. Numerous international agencies, including some from the United Nations, began adopting her development models for use in other countries. She and those working with her were active partners in implementing the same kinds of projects in other Arab nations.

THE HORRIFIC PROBLEM OF HONOR KILLINGS

In connection with her work for women's rights, Queen Noor has outspokenly addressed the problem of "honor killings." These are the murders of women by male relatives who feel the woman has acted in a way that shames the family. These killings occur in countries throughout the Middle East and in other parts of the Muslim and non-Muslim world. Even being raped may bring murder upon a girl or woman. In extreme cases, the victim may be killed for something as minor as talking to a man who is not a relative. The murderers usually receive only light sentences, such as a few weeks or months in jail, if that. It is not uncommon for a man to walk away free.

In Jordan, honor killing has yet to be outlawed. People have made efforts to change this, but the male population of Jordan (as well as some other Arab nations) won't budge. Attempts to make punishment for honor killings equal to that for other murders, Noor reports, "have been resisted over many, many years by conservative members of parliament. . . . [We] are talking about a very small number of killings [in Jordan there were 19 in 2001 and 22 in 2002] but none of them are acceptable. . . . There are so many patriarchal patterns that run counter to Islam. Islam forbids taking the law into one's own hands, and it forbids the kind of slander that often comes with condemning these women." But here, too, tradition wins the day.

Today, King Abdullah's wife, Queen Rania, is Jordan's official spokesperson against these horrific crimes. Like Queen Noor, she continues to fight on behalf of Islamic women.

Throughout all her efforts, one of Queen Noor's greatest goals is to build partnerships that will lead to peace. And when she speaks out for people with little power, she always emphasizes the benefits of including women in the conversation. The kinds of partnerships she envisions, Noor points out, "especially need the people whose human rights and potential have been most ignored—women."

NEGATIVE STEREOTYPES

Related to the issue of women's rights is the issue of negative Arab and Muslim stereotypes. Westerners tend to believe that all Muslim women are oppressed, for example, while this is far from true. It is yet another stereotype. Queen Noor is an excellent case in point. And she is all about changing these attitudes and erroneous beliefs.

"As a humanitarian activist, I try to provide a voice, where I can, for people who don't yet have a voice," she told an interviewer in 2003. "So many Arabs and Muslims are struggling with the ignorance, prejudice, and fear that seem to prevail about our religion and culture. I try to be a voice for the true value of Islam and Arab culture. . . . [U]nfortunately, the actions of a small minority of terrorists or violent extremists have become the lens through which much of the world looks at the Arab and Muslim world."

Being a part of both cultures—Middle Eastern and western— Noor can dispel stereotypes more effectively than someone who has lived only in one region or the other. "She's got a tough sell telling Americans that the U.S. and Islam should have good relations," Queen Noor's longtime friend Jean AbiNader stated to *People* magazine. AbiNader is a founding board member of the Arab American Institute. "She really does embody this bridge between the U.S. and the Arab world," he added.

LOOKING TO THE MOVIES

Queen Noor is passionate about the idea of promoting peace by bringing about understanding among cultures. And one way to broaden the West's understanding of Middle Eastern peoples and culture, she believes, is through the power of film. These ideas fuel Noor's outreach to the film industry, which began as early as 1980.

That year, on her first official state visit to the United States with King Hussein, Noor met with Hollywood film industry leaders. Her aim, she notes in her memoir, was to "explore ways that Hollywood might . . . [convey] a more balanced and realistic portrayal" of Muslims and Arabs.

"The images Hollywood has created . . . and exported throughout the world certainly do not promote mutual respect," Queen Noor told an audience who came to hear her speak in Washington, D.C. "A very diverse population has been pigeonholed into a few stereotypes: Oil-rich sheiks in a region where many live in poverty; bloodthirsty aggressors instead of the refugees whose homes and lands have been taken from them; ignorant fanatics—in fact a tiny minority in a land of many cultured, educated professionals; cloistered oppressed women instead of the doctors, lawyers, government ministers, and businesswomen I know and work with; and now the poor and downtrodden who need to be rescued from their own culture, rather than the proud and patriotic people entitled to freedom and self-determination." Queen Noor's visit with the Hollywood moguls did not have much result. But, she says, "trying to put a human face on the plight of the Palestinians and presenting a counterpoint to the stereotypical depictions of Arabs and Muslims in the movies would become a theme of my married life."

Noor has not given up since her first try twenty years ago. And these days her message is spreading more successfully. She has found much more receptivity throughout Hollywood and says she feels encouraged by the progress she sees.

In December 2009 Queen Noor gave a keynote speech at the sixth annual Dubai Film Festival. She talked about the humiliation, conflict, and misunderstanding that negative stereotypes can cause. Then she noted that the media has the power "to touch us in profound ways, to challenge our preconceived notions, open our hearts, and maybe even our minds." This time, unlike in earlier decades, the Hollywood producers the queen was addressing heard her message loud and clear.

Noor began speaking out on this matter long ago. As a young queen beginning to accept public speaking engagements, she was not shy about expressing her opinions. "I felt a strong responsibility, almost a moral obligation," she has said, "to try to correct grossly distorted Western stereotypes of Arabs and Muslims, especially women."

Queen Noor noticed that the media only rarely portrayed the kind, friendly, moderate types of Muslims she knew. And the same media hardly ever mentioned the millions who were suffering greatly as a result of Middle Eastern conflicts. Noor realized that "media stereotyping could set the emotional and political stage for policies that resulted in chronic misunderstanding, suffering, and conflict." This left her feeling "anger and frustration about the gulf of ignorance and fear separating both worlds."

YOUTH MAKE ALL THE DIFFERENCE

Queen Noor is well aware that young people have incredible power to change things. They can go into the world with a new and enlightened vision—and thereby change old, worn-out attitudes, ideas, and prejudices. Sometimes it can even happen more rapidly than one might think—especially when people look past cultural differences and see the underlying human unity that King Hussein and Queen Noor saw. "We must speak out against those who promote a clash of cultures," Noor says. "Ours must be a voice of reason . . . of solidarity and of hope."

Around the world young people are hearing the call. Queen Noor continues to reach out to youth in multiple ways. "[Y]oung people today have access to so much information that it is difficult to process what is useful, accurate, and current. At the same time, they have the advantage of instant access and can reach out to better understand the differences," she told an interviewer for a young people's magazine. "By reaching out, they can enrich their understanding of each other. People around the world—young and old—share a yearning for peace, for opportunity, and for jobs that can fulfill their talents. . . . These shared yearnings can help to bring us closer together."

Today Queen Noor's dream of helping people and making the world a better place has been richly fulfilled. But she hasn't slowed down. She is as involved as ever in promoting good on Earth. And she is optimistic about inspiring young people around the globe to do the same. Anyone can get the message and act on it. She points out,

> **One thing King Hussein himself proved and that we've seen throughout history, is that one person can make an extraordinary difference in the world. If that difference helps others, it doesn't matter what position you are in—king or student in school. . . . In Islam there is a Golden Rule: 'No one of you is a believer until he wishes for his brother what he wishes for himself.' If you live your life according to this rule, you can have a profound impact on the world.**

TIMELINE

1951 — Lisa Najeeb Halaby born in Washington, D.C., on August 23.

1969 — Graduates from high school; enters Princeton University as part of its first coed class.

1971 — Drops out of Princeton to work in Aspen, Colorado; works with the nonprofit Aspen Institute and discovers an interest in architecture and urban planning.

1974 — Graduates from Princeton University; travels to Australia, where she works with an architectural firm.

1975 — Moves to Tehran, Iran, to work on a major architecture and urban planning project for the shah of Iran.

1976 — Travels to Jordan for the first time in the spring. Returns in the fall with her father and first meets King Hussein.

1978 — After a brief courtship, marries King Hussein of Jordan on June 15 and becomes his fourth wife. Accepts the new name of Noor Al Hussein, or Light of Hussein.

1979 — Suffers a miscarriage. Establishes the Royal Endowment for Culture and Education.

1980 — Gives birth to her first child, Hamzah, on March 29. Takes first state visit to the United States since marriage.

1981 — Accepts a speaking engagement at Georgetown University in Washington, D.C., her first public political speech. Gives birth to Hashim, her second son, on June 10. Establishes the Jerash Festival of Culture and Arts in October in Amman, Jordan.

1983 — Gives birth to daughter Iman on April 24.

1985	Establishes the Noor Al Hussein Foundation (NHF), whose mission is to expand opportunities for Jordanians in a broad range of areas.
1986	Gives birth to her last child, daughter Raiyah, on February 9.
1992	Travels with King Hussein to the Mayo Clinic in Minnesota after doctors find precancerous cells in the ureter leading to one of the king's kidneys. As a precaution, he undergoes surgery for the removal of the kidney.
1993	Establishes the Jubilee School, a secondary school aimed at developing academic and leadership excellence in outstanding students.
1995	On June 5, receives UN Environmental Program Global 500 Award for "activism in environmental protection, in promoting awareness and in initiating community action for the preservation of Jordan's natural heritage."
1998	King Hussein diagnosed with non-Hodgkin's lymphoma.
1999	King Hussein dies on February 7 in Jordan. King Hussein Foundation (KHF) established. King Hussein's son Abdullah becomes king of Jordan.
2002	*Vogue* magazine declares Noor one of the world's 100 Most Glamorous Women.
2003	Publishes best-selling memoir, *Leap of Faith: Memoirs of an Unexpected Life.*
2009	In March, Harvard's Center for Health and the Global Environment awards its Global Environmental Citizen award to Queen Noor for her outstanding contributions to environmentalism.

In July, as chairperson of the King Hussein Foundation, Queen Noor participates in a weeklong series of events commemorating the foundation's tenth anniversary.

In December, Queen Noor delivers keynote address at the Dubai International Film Festival.

SOURCE NOTES

Boxed quotes unless otherwise noted

CHAPTER 1

p. 5, par. 2, "29th International Arab Children's Congress Focuses on Children's Security," www.kinghusseinfoundation.org/index.php?pager= end&type=news&task=view&pageid=44

p. 7, sidebar par. 1, Namrouqa, Hana. "Annual Children's Congress Opens Today." *Jordan Times*, July 5, 2009. www.jordantimes.com/?news=18123

p. 8, sidebar par. 2, "The Hashemites," Background Note: Jordan. U.S. Department of State. www.state.gov/r/pa/ei/bgn/3464.htm

p. 8, sidebar par. 3, "Disengagement From the West Bank." History section, Jordan/King Hussein official government site. www.kinghussein.gov.jo/ his_periods9.html

p. 8, sidebar par. 3, Glassman, Carl. "Jordan's American Queen Speaks Out." *Senior Scholastic,* April 17, 1981, p. 13.

CHAPTER 2

p. 11, par. 2, Noor Al Hussein. *Leap of Faith: Memoirs of an Unexpected Life.* (New York: Miramax Books, 2003), p. 20 [paperback].

p. 17, Noor, *Leap of Faith*, p. 19.

p. 17, par. 2, Noor, *Leap of Faith*, p. 20.

p. 20, Noor, *Leap of Faith*, p. 26.

p. 23, sidebar, Noor, *Leap of Faith*, p. 23.

CHAPTER 3

p. 26, par. 3 [3rd full par.], Lafferty, Elaine. "Queen Noor: The Next Chapter." *Ms.*, Fall, 2003, p.34-39.

p. 28, sidebar par. 2, Caputo, Philip. *A Rumor of War: Marine Officer in Vietnam.* (New York: Holt, Rinehart and Winston, 1977). Quotes found at Learn History: Conflict in Vietnam 1954-1975. www.learnhistory.org. uk/vietnam/coursework.htm

p. 28, sidebar par. 3, Hickman, Kennedy. "Vietnam War: End of the Conflict,

1973-1975." About.com: Military History. http://militaryhistory.about.
com/od/vietnamwar/a/VietnamEnd.htm

p. 29, Noor, *Leap of Faith*, p. 33.

p. 31, par. 1, Noor, *Leap of Faith*, p. 34.

p. 31, par. 2, Fernandez, Tom. "1969: Going coed with guts and grace."
Trentonian. www.capitalcentury.com/1969.html

p. 32, sidebar par. 1, Noor, *Leap of Faith*, p. 28.

p. 34, Noor, *Leap of Faith*, p. 38.

p. 35, sidebar par.1, Dunne, Dominick. "The Light of Hussein." *Vanity Fair.*
January 1991, p. 114.

p. 35, sidebar par. 2, Pesta, Abigail. "More Than a Pretty Face: Queen Noor of
Jordan." *Marie Claire.* January 2008, p. 70.

p. 36, Noor, *Leap of Faith*, p. 39.

p. 36, Noor, *Leap of Faith*, p. 40.

p. 37, par. 1, "The Iranian Revolution." Washington State University. http://
wsu.edu/~dee/SHIA/REV.HTM.

p. 37, par. 4, Noor, *Leap of Faith*, p. 45.

CHAPTER 4

p. 39, par. 1, Noor, *Leap of Faith*, p. 8.

p. 41, par. 2, Noor, *Leap of Faith*, p. 48.

p. 42, Dunne, Dominick. "The Light of Hussein." *Vanity Fair*, January 1991, p.
61-62.

CHAPTER 5

p. 48, par. 1, The Family Tree of His Majesty King Hussein of Jordan. www.
kinghussein.gov.jo/rfamily_hashemites.html

p. 48, par. 2, Biographical Information: Abdullah bin al-Hussein. www.
kinghussein.gov.jo/kingabdullah.html

p. 49, par. 4, Address to the Summit of the Peacemakers, Sharm el-Sheikh,
Egypt, March 13, 1996. www.kinghussein.gov.jo/96_march13.html

p. 50, par. 5 [full], Noor, *Leap of Faith*, p. 97.

p. 51, line 1, Noor, *Leap of Faith*, p. 98.

p. 51, par. 2, Noor, *Leap of Faith*, p. 103.

p. 54, Noor, *Leap of Faith*, p. 99.

p. 54, sidebar par. 1, Who is Toujan al-Faisal? Virtual Activism website. http://toujan.virtualactivism.net/about.htm.

p. 54, sidebar par. 1, Viorst, Milton. "The House of Hashem." *New Yorker,* January 7, 1991, p. 50.

p. 54, sidebar par. 2, Viorst, *New Yorker,* p. 50.

p. 55, par. 1, Saad, Najwa. "Queen Noor on 'the power of people with faith to accomplish change.'" *Washington Report on Middle East Affairs.* 24.4 (May-June 2005).

p. 55, Pesta, Abigail. "More Than a Pretty Face: Queen Noor of Jordan," p. 70.

p. 56, par. 2, Dunne, *Vanity Fair,* p.64.

p. 56, Noor, *Leap of Faith*, p. 91.

p. 57, Noor, *Leap of Faith*, p. 91-92.

p. 57, par. 2, Noor, *Leap of Faith*, p. 141.

CHAPTER 6

p. 59, Noor, *Leap of Faith*, p. 150.

p. 60, Noor, *Leap of Faith*, p. 148.

p. 60, par. 4 [through P. 61, 1st par.], O'Shaughnessy, Elise. "The American Queen: She left the U.S. and adopted a new faith, to marry a king..." Real Lives section, *Good Housekeeping,* April 2003, p. 125 (3).

p. 61, Queen Noor of Jordan. Speech at the Kennedy Center for the Performing Arts, March 4, 1996. Gifts of Speech. http://gos.sbc.edu/n/noor3.html

p. 62, Glassman, Carl. "Jordan's American Queen Speaks Out." *Senior Scholastic,* April 17, 1981, p. 12.

p. 62, par. 3 [through p. 63, p. 1], Dunne, *Vanity Fair,* p. 64.

p. 63, par. 1 [complete], Noor, *Leap of Faith*, p. 130.

p. 64, par. 1, O'Connor, Mickey. "Her Majesty Queen Noor of Jordan." *Architecture,* March 2000, p. 40.

p. 64, par. 2, Noor, *Leap of Faith*, p. 164.

p. 65, Noor, *Leap of Faith*, p. 260.

p. 66, sidebar par. 2, Noor, *Leap of Faith*, p. 164.

p. 67, par. 1, National Music Conservatory." KHF Institutions. King Hussein

Foundation. www.kinghusseinfoundation.org/index.php?pager=end&task= view&type=content&pageid=41

p. 67, par. 1, Noor, *Leap of Faith*, p. 259.

p. 67, Queen Noor, "Coalitions: We Must Join Together for Peace." *Vital Speeches of the Day,* vol. LXIX, no. 22. September 1, 2003, p. 676. (Speech delivered to the Meridian Club, Washington, D.C., 5/24/03).

p. 68, par. 1, Queen Noor, *Vital Speeches of the Day,* p. 676.

p. 68, par. 2, Jerash Festival of Culture and Arts. July 1, 2009 – August 30, 2009 http://business.maktoob.com/20090000000072/ArticleEvents.htm

p. 69, sidebar par. 3, Queen Noor of Jordan. "Obama's Opportunity to Lead a Landmine-Free World." *Huffington Post.* December 3, 2009. www.huffingtonpost.com/her-majesty-queen-noor/obamas-opportunity-to-lea_b_379091.html

p. 70, par. 1, Busé, Margaret S. "Her Majesty Queen Noor of Jordan: A Commitment to Landmine Awareness and Victim and Survivor Assistance." Focus on Victim and Survivor Assistance, Journal of Mine Action. Mine Action Information Center at James Madison University. Fall 1999. vol. 3, no. 3. http://maic.jmu.edu/Journal/3.3/focus/queen_noor.htm

p. 70, Busé, Margaret S. *Journal of Mine Action.* Fall 1999. vol. 3, no. 3. http://maic.jmu.edu/Journal/3.3/focus/queen_noor.htm

p. 70, Noor, *Leap of Faith*, p. 251.

p. 72, sidebar par. 1, Noor Al Hussein Foundation. www.nooralhusseinfoundation.org

p. 72, sidebar par. 2, Queen Noor of Jordan. Gifts of Speech, http://gos.sbc.edu/n/noor3.html

p. 72, sidebar par. 3, Queen Noor of Jordan. Gifts of Speech, http://gos.sbc.edu/n/noor3.html

CHAPTER 7

p. 76, par. 2, Noor, *Leap of Faith*, p. 63.

p. 76, par. 3, Noor, *Leap of Faith*, p. 61.

p. 77, sidebar par. 1, The Balfour Declaration 1917. www.adespicabletruce.org.uk/page68.html

p. 78, Noor, *Leap of Faith*, p. 65.

p. 79, Noor, *Leap of Faith*, p. 66.

p. 80, sidebar, "The Disaster of 1967." History section, Jordan/King Hussein official government site. www.kinghussein.gov.jo/his_periods3.html; "1967: Israel Launches Attack on Egypt." On This Day, 1950-2005: 5 June. BBC News. http://news.bbc.co.uk/onthisday/hi/dates/stories/june/5/ newsid_2654000/2654251.stm

p. 80, sidebar par. 3, "In 1967 Israel did not wake up one morning and decide to go to war - she woke up one morning and found she had to defend herself." Sixdaywar.co.uk. www.sixdaywar.co.uk/

p. 81, par. 2, Palestine Facts: "Israel 1967-1991. Jordan Expels PLO." www. palestinefacts.org/pf_1967to1991_jordan_expel_plo.php

p. 82, par. 1, Pesta, *Marie Claire*, January 2008, p. 70.

p. 83, sidebar par. 1, Viorst, *New Yorker*, January 7, 1991, p. 41.

p. 83, par. 1, Pesta, *Marie Claire*, January 2008, p. 70.

p. 84, par. 1, Noor, *Leap of Faith*, p. 215.

p. 84, Noor, *Leap of Faith*, p. 214.

p. 85, Queen Noor, *Vital Speeches of the Day*, p. 676.

CHAPTER 8

p. 88, line 2 (partial paragraph), Noor, *Leap of Faith*, p. 158.

p. 88, first [full] par., line 3, Noor, *Leap of Faith*, p. 158.

p. 88, Noor, *Leap of Faith*, p. 185.

p. 90, Noor, *Leap of Faith*, p. 182.

p. 91, Noor, *Leap of Faith*, p. 182.

p. 92, sidebar, Noor, *Leap of Faith*, p. 173.

p. 93, par. 3, Noor, *Leap of Faith*, p. 177.

p. 93, Noor, *Leap of Faith*, p. 177.

p. 95, par. 1, "Iran-Iraq War (1980-1988)." Global Security.org. www. globalsecurity.org/military/world/war/iran-iraq.htm

p. 96, par. 3, Noor, *Leap of Faith*, p. 314-15.

p. 97, Dunne, *Vanity Fair*, January 1990, p.114.

p. 97, par. 1, Dunne, *Vanity Fair*, January 1990, p.114.

p. 98, par. 1, Noor, *Leap of Faith*, p. 315.

p. 98, par. 2, Noor, *Leap of Faith*, p. 315.

p. 98, par. 2, Noor, *Leap of Faith*, p. 349.

p. 99, sidebar par. 2, Noor, *Leap of Faith*, p. 417.

p. 100, par. 1, Noor, *Leap of Faith*, p. 412-413.

p. 100, Noor, *Leap of Faith*, p. 441.

p. 100, par. 5, Noor, *Leap of Faith*, p. 441.

p. 103, par. 1 [partial], Noor, *Leap of Faith*, p. 443.

p. 103, par. 1 [full], Noor, *Leap of Faith*, p. 444.

CHAPTER 9

p. 106, sidebar par. 2, "About Us." King Hussein Foundation. [Both quotes in this paragraph.] www.kinghusseinfoundation.org/index.php?pager=end&task=view&type=content&pageid=1

p. 106, par. 2, Lafferty, *Ms.*, fall 2003, p. 36.

p. 107, par. 3, Baker, Rosalie F. "Queen Noor: Interview with Her Majesty." *Faces: People, Places, and Cultures.* November 2003, p. 22-25.

p. 107, par. 4, Queen Noor of Jordan, Gifts of Speech, http://gos.sbc.edu/n/noor3.html.

p. 108, sidebar par. 2, Lafferty, *Ms.*, fall, 2003, p. 36.

p. 108, sidebar par. 2, Pesta, *Marie Claire.* January 2008, p. 70.

p. 109, par. 1, Queen Noor. *Vital Speeches of the Day*, Vol. LXIX, September 1, 2003, p. 676.

p. 109, par. 3, Baker, *Faces: People, Places, and Cultures.* November 2003, p. 22-25.

p. 109, par. 4, Espinoza, Galina. "A New Realm: Emerging from grief, Jordan's Queen Noor writes a bestselling memoir." *People Weekly,* June 9, 2003. p. 115.

p. 112, par. 1, Queen Noor of Jordan. Gifts of Speech, http://gos.sbc.edu/n/noor3.html

p. 112, par. 2, Queen Noor of Jordan. Gifts of Speech, http://gos.sbc.edu/n/noor3.html.

p. 112, par. 3, Assaf, Roxanne. "Jordan's Former Queen Graces Podium in America's Arab-American Hub." *Washington Report on Middle East Affairs.* March 2002, p. 93.

p. 113, par. 1 [partial], Baker, *Faces: People, Places, and Cultures.* November 2003, p. 22-25.

p. 113, Baker, *Faces: People, Places, and Cultures.* November 2003, p. 22-25.

FURTHER INFORMATION

BOOKS

Davenport, John. *A Brief Political and Geographic History of the Middle East.* Hockessin, DE: Mitchell Lane Publishers, 2008.

Downing, David. *The Making of the Middle East.* Chicago: Raintree, 2006.

Raatma, Lucia. *Queen Noor: American-Born Queen of Jordan.* Minneapolis: Compass Point Books, 2006.

South, Coleman. *Jordan* (Cultures of the World). New York: Marshall Cavendish, 2008.

WEBSITES

King Hussein Foundation
www.kinghusseinfoundation.org
This humanitarian nonprofit organization's official website provides information on the numerous new and ongoing projects the King Hussein Foundation is engaged in.

Noor Al Hussein Foundation
www.nooralhusseinfoundation.org
The official website of the humanitarian nonprofit organization the Noor Al Hussein Foundation, which focuses on community development projects that provide economic benefit to underprivileged communities.

BIBLIOGRAPHY

BOOKS

Caputo, Philip. *A Rumor of War: Marine Officer in Vietnam.* New York: Holt, Rinehart and Winston, 1977. Quotations found at "Learn History: Conflict in Vietnam 1954–1975," www.learnhistory.org.uk/vietnam/coursework.htm

Noor Al Hussein. *Leap of Faith: Memoirs of an Unexpected Life.* London: Orion Books, Ltd., 2003.

PERIODICALS

Assaf, Roxanne. "Jordan's Former Queen Graces Podium in America's Arab-American Hub." *Washington Report on Middle East Affairs*, March 2002, p. 93.

Baker, Rosalie F. "Queen Noor: Interview with Her Majesty." *Faces: People, Places, and Cultures*, November 2003, p. 22 (4).

Dunne, Dominick. "The Light of Hussein." *Vanity Fair*, January 1991, p. 114.

Espinoza, Galina. "A New Realm: Emerging from Grief, Jordan's Queen Noor Writes a Bestselling Memoir." *People Weekly*, June 9, 2003, p. 115.

Glassman, Carl. "Jordan's American Queen Speaks Out." *Senior Scholastic*, April 17, 1981, p. 13.

Lafferty, Elaine. "Queen Noor: The Next Chapter." *Ms.*, fall 2003, pp. 34–39.

Noor Al Hussein. "Coalitions: We Must Join Together for Peace." *Vital Speeches of the Day*, vol. LXIX, no. 22, September 1, 2003, p. 676. (Speech delivered to the Meridian Club, Washington, D.C., 5/24/03.)

O'Connor, Mickey. "Her Majesty Queen Noor of Jordan." *Architecture*, March 2000, p. 40.

O'Shaughnessy, Elise. "The American Queen: She Left the U.S. and Adopted a New Faith, to Marry a King." *Good Housekeeping*, April 2003, p. 125 (3).

Pesta, Abigail. "More Than a Pretty Face: Queen Noor of Jordan." *Marie Claire*, January 2008, p. 70.

Saad, Najwa. "Queen Noor on 'the Power of People with Faith to Accomplish Change.'" *Washington Report on Middle East Affairs*, vol. 24, no. 4, May–June 2005, p. 67 (2).

Viorst, Milton. "The House of Hashem." *New Yorker*, January 7, 1991, p. 37.

WEBSITES

"About Us." King Hussein Foundation. www.kinghusseinfoundation.org/index.php?pager=end&task=view&type=content&pageid=1

Biographical Information: Abdullah bin al-Hussein. www.kinghussein.gov.jo/kingabdullah.html

Busé, Margaret S. "Her Majesty Queen Noor of Jordan: A Commitment to Landmine Awareness and Victim and Survivor Assistance." Focus on Victim and Survivor Assistance, *Journal of Mine Action*. Mine Action Information Center at James Madison University, fall 1999, vol. 3, no. 3. www.maic.jmu.edu/Journal/3.3/focus/queen_noor.htm

The Family Tree of His Majesty King Hussein of Jordan. www.kinghussein.gov.jo/rfamily_hashemites.html

Fernandez, Tom. "1969: Going Coed with Guts and Grace." *Trentonian*. www.capitalcentury.com/1969.html

"H.M. Queen Noor Delivers Keynote Speech at the Dubai International Film Festival on the Power of Film to Bridge the Culture Gaps." December 13, 2009. King Hussein Foundation. www.kinghusseinfoundation.org/index.php?pager=end&type=news&task=view&pageid=44 "29th International Arab Children's Congress Focuses on Children's Security." King Hussein Foundation. www.kinghusseinfoundation.org/index.php?pager=end&type=news&task=view&pageid=44

Hussein bin Talal. "Address to the Summit of the Peacemakers, Sharm el-Sheikh, Egypt, March 13, 1996." www.kinghussein.gov.jo/96_march13.html

"Iran-Iraq War (1980-1988)." www.globalsecurity.org/military/world/war/iran-iraq.htm

"Jerash Festival Comes to an End." April 5, 2008. www.thefreelibrary.com/
Jerash+Festival+comes+to+an+end-a0178592797

"Jerash." Ruth's Jordan Jubilee. www.jordanjubilee.com/visitjor/jerash.htm

"National Music Conservatory." KHF Institutions. King Hussein Foundation.
www.kinghusseinfoundation.org/index.php?pager=end&task=view&typ
e=content&pageid=41

Noor Al Hussein. "Speech at the Kennedy Center for the Performing Arts,
March 4, 1996." Gifts of Speech. www.gos.sbc.edu/n/noor3.html

Noor Al Hussein. "Obama's Opportunity to Lead a Landmine-Free World."
Huffington Post, December 3, 2009. www.huffingtonpost.com/her-
majesty-queen-noor/obamas-opportunity-to-lea_b_379091.html

Palestine Facts. "Israel 1967–1991. Jordan Expels PLO." www.
palestinefacts.org/pf_1967to1991_jordan_expel_plo.php

Toujan al-Faisal website, detailing the life, background, and apostasy case of
Toujan al-Faisal, the first woman elected to the Jordanian parliament.
See www.toujan.virtualactivism.net/about.htm

INDEX

Abdullah I, 8, 48
Abdullah II, 100, 102
al-Faisal, Toujan, 54-55
Alia, Queen, 40, 42-43
Al-Ma'wa, 57
Amman, Jordan, 5, 7, 38, 40-41, 100
Arab Air Services, 40
Arab American Institute, 109
Arab Children's Congress, 93
Arab culture. See Islam
Arabic language, 90-91
Arab-Israeli conflict, 48, 75-78, 79-81
Arab stereotypes, 83, 85, 105, 109-112
Arab Summit Conference of 1980, 7
architecture, 31, 33, 37
Aspen Institute, 30-31, 33
Australia, 31, 33
autobiography, 21
awards and recognitions, 104, 105

Balfour Declaration, 76, 77
Bani Hamida Women's Weaving Project, 107
British control in Middle East, 75-76

Camp David Accords, 94
Carlquist, Doris, 11-12
Carter, Jimmy, 94
celebrity, adapting to, 59-62
Center for Contemporary Arab Studies, 83-84
Chapin School, 21-22, 23, 32
childhood, 11-13, 14, 17, 18-19
children
    Jordanian, aiding, 64-67, 83, 93
    of Queen Noor, 87-90, 89
Children's Heritage and Science Museum, 67
civil rights movement, U.S., 18-19, 22, 29
clothing, traditional, 35, 36
college education, 25-27, 30, 31
Concord Academy, 22-23, 32
constitution of Jordan, 8, 48
cultural initiatives, 65, 67, 68

Dina, Queen, 43

education
    in Jordan, 64-65, 83, 91
    of Queen Noor, 17, 21-23, 25-26, 31, 32

Egypt, 49, 80, 94, 96
elections, in Jordan, 8, 48
employment, of Queen Noor, 30, 31, 33-34, 39, 40
environmental protection, 64, 68

fashion, 59-61
Federal Aviation Administration (FAA), 14-15
Fuller, Buckminster, 30

gender issues. See women
Georgetown University, 83-84
Great Arab Revolt, 75

Halaby, Laura, 14, 17
Halaby, Najeeb "Jeeb," 11-15, 15, 16, 18, 20-21, 39
Harrow School, England, 49
Hashemite Kingdom of Jordan. See Jordan
Hashimya Palace, Amman, 41
head scarves, 35
health care, 64-65, 81-82
honor killings, 108
Hussein, King
    courtship, 40-41, 44-45, 47
    death and funeral, 100-101, 101
    health problems, 98-99
    peacemaking efforts, 87, 94, 96-97
    personal life, 42-43, 48-49, 98
Hussein, Saddam, 93

International Arab Children's Congress (IACC), 4, 5, 7
International Campaign to Ban Landmines (ICBL), 70
Iran, 33-37, 69, 94-96
Iran-Iraq war, 94-96
Iraq, 6, 74, 75, 82, 94-96
Islam, 35, 36, 50-51, 54-55, 108
Israel, 6, 48, 76, 77
    as aggressor, 78-79, 80
    peace negotiations, 81, 84, 94

Jerash Festival of Culture and Arts, 68
Johnson, Lyndon B., 16, 20
Jordan
    demographics of, 64
    refugees and, 78, 80, 82, 96
    geography of, 6
    history and politics of, 8, 48-49, 75, 102

peace negotiations and, 94
PLO and, 79, 81
Six-Day War and, 80
Jordan Festival, 68

Kennedy, John F., 14–15, 15, 20
Kent State University shootings, 29
King, Martin Luther, Jr., 19
King Hussein Foundation, 105, 106
Kuwait, 82, 96–97

land mines, 68–70
Landmine Survivors Network, 70
Leap of Faith: Memoirs of an Unexpected Life (Queen Noor), 21
Llewelyn-Davies Weeks, 33, 37

marriage and honeymoon, 51–52, 53, 56
Meredith, James, 19
Muna, Princess, 43, 43
music, as cultural initiative, 65

names, Queen Noor and, 42–43, 51, 52, 56
National Cathedral School, 17
National Coalition for Children, 67
National Committee for Public Buildings and Architectural Heritage, 64
National Committee for the Child, 64
National Handicrafts Development program, 107
National Music Conservatory (NMC), 65
Noor Al Hussein Foundation (NHF), 70, 72, 82–83, 107

Obama, Barack, 69
Ottawa Mine Ban Treaty, 69

Palestine, 48, 76–81, 111
peace negotiations and, 84, 94
Queen Alia and, 42
refugees from, 78–79, 80, 96
Palestinian Liberation Organization (PLO), 79, 81
Pan-American Airlines, 21
Peace Corps, 17, 18
Persian Gulf War, 96
personal life
adapting to celebrity, 50–51, 59–62
childhood, 11–13, 14, 17, 18–19
courtship, 40–41, 44–45, 47
Islam and, 50–51, 63, 101, 103
learning Arabic, 90–91

motherhood, 87–90, 89
shyness and public speaking, 13–14, 15, 83–85
wedding, 51–52, 53
political activism, 26–29
Princeton University, 25–26, 30, 31, 32
privacy, 93

Qaddafi, Muammar, 92, 93

Rania, Queen, 102, 108
refugees, 78, 80, 81–83, 82, 96
Royal Endowment for Culture and Education, 91
Royal Military Academy, Sandhurst, England, 49, 92
Royal Society for the Conservation of Nature (RSCN), 68

Sadat, Anwar, 94
shyness and public speaking, 13–14, 15, 83–85
Six-Day War, 80
social conscience, development of, 11, 15, 17, 18–19
SOS Children's Villages, 65, 66
SOS Kinderhof International, 66
stereotypes, 83, 85, 105, 109–112
Student Nonviolent Coordinating Committee, 18
Summit of the Peacemakers, 49
Syria, 6, 75, 80, 94

Talal, King, 49
Tehran, Iran, 33–34, 34, 36–37
Timeline, 114–115
Transjordan, 48, 78

United Nations World Summit for Children, 67
United States, invasion of Iraq and, 82

vaccines, 64
Victoria College, Egypt, 49
Vietnam War, 22, 26–27, 27, 28, 29

women
empowerment, 92, 106–107, 109
role as celebrity, 59–62
role in Islam, 35, 36, 54–55, 108

youth, political involvement of, 5, 7, 67, 83, 112–113

ABOUT THE AUTHOR

PAMELA DELL is the author of more than sixty books for children and young people. These works include an award-winning twelve-book series for Encyclopedia Britannica titled Britannica Discovery Library as well as books about nature, history, and geography and numerous biographies. She is also the author of Scrapbooks of America, a twelve-book series of historical fiction. Pamela divides her time between Los Angeles and Chicago.